INTEGRATING ACQUISITIONS

INTEGRATING ACQUISITIONS

MAKING CORPORATE MARRIAGES WORK

JAMES A. YUNKER

PRAEGER SPECIAL STUDIES • PRAEGER SCIENTIFIC

New York • Philadelphia • Eastbourne, UK
Toronto • Hong Kong • Tokyo • Sydney

Library of Congress Cataloging in Publication Data

Yunker, James A.
    Integrating acquisitions.

    Includes index.
    1. Consolidation and merger of corporations. I. Title.
HD2746.5.Y86   1983   658.1'6   83-13871
ISBN 0-03-069314-4

Published in 1983 by Praeger Publishers
CBS Educational and Professional Publishing
a Division of CBS Inc.
521 Fifth Avenue, New York, New York 10175 U.S.A.

3456789 052   987654321

Printed in the United States of America
on acid-free paper

ACKNOWLEDGMENTS

THE AUTHOR has many people to thank for helpful interest during the process of transforming his ideas into this book.

Most important have been Professors James and Penelope Yunker of Western Illinois University, whose advice and encouragement throughout the project were of critical importance. Also James Sowers, General Instrument Corporation financial executive, who made valuable comments and suggestions concerning the financial systems and integrating data processing chapters.

Jan Spitzer, manager of home office in Evanston, Illinois, and her associates diligently and carefully transcribed a barely legible handwritten manuscript into finished typed form.

Finally, a very special kind of gratitude is due my wife, Margaret, for her affection and support through all the thirty-five years required to obtain the experiences encapsulated in this work.

CONTENTS

INTEGRATING ACQUISITIONS

1
INTRODUCTION

ANY BUSINESS ENTERPRISE contains within itself all the elements of human drama. Struggle, triumphs, failures, hopes, humor, even tragedy are all to be found in the complex endeavor known as the business corporation.

All these ingredients emerge in their starkest form in the acquisition situation. When one company buys another, the interactions between their people, the conflict of personalities, of ideas, the tensions and frustrations inherent in business life reach a peak. The difficulties that are a normal part of corporate life are badly exacerbated by the new relationships.

Yet if the acquired company is to meet the expectations of its new parent corporation, and if the acquired personnel are to take their place as valued contributors to its success, the very real problems of the after-acquisition situation must be overcome.

This book provides realistic guidance for the millions of business people who have been or will be involved with new corporate entities, whether as acquirer or acquiree, in how to handle the numerous obstacles that *will* arise. The method is to describe the problems and then to present suggestions for avoiding or minimizing their harmful effects.

The text also provides perceptive readers with numerous examples of what to do and what to avoid as they progress through various corporate levels and functions. These are presented in the context of achieving good working relationships between the staff and line people of a multi-division corporation. The complications involved in successfully integrating an acquired company also exist in the day-to-day operations of any business enterprise, though usually not in as dramatic a form.

Business students also will find useful insights throughout the book whatever their major, as activities in planning and administration as well as the line functions are discussed. The differences that distinguish good operating practice from bad are illustrated in every chapter.

Finally, today there is an increasing awareness among the general public that healthy and varied business activity is a critical element in maintaining an economically successful United States. This has led to increased interest in how companies really operate and make their decisions. This text can be read with understanding by anyone not directly engaged in business but curious about the working processes of business enterprise.

The style is conversational and anecdotal, illustrating the points discussed with realistic and understandable situations and protagonists. Though the subject is a serious one, the text also recognizes that there is humor in business, frequently unintended.

A large, multi-division corporation acquires a smaller company. The acquisition is entered into with high hopes. It is expected that the new entity will make valuable contribution to the overall corporate welfare. The acquired company has been successful in its field, perhaps the leader. It extends the larger corporation's range into promising product and technology fields. The future looks bright.

Then, all too often, following consummation of the corporate marriage, the high expectations are not realized. Within a very short period, even a year or two, somehow things have gone wrong. The formerly independent company, now a division of the larger corporation, isn't doing what it was supposed to do. Financial and market penetration goals are not being met. New product programs are behind schedule. Dissatisfied customers are becoming more numerous. There has been a heavy turnover in its executive ranks. Relationships between the division and headquarters people have soured. Mutual recriminations fill the air.

What happened?

It is the argument of this book that most of the problems so often adversely affecting the performance of a new acquisition are internally generated by the acquirers and by the new entity. The wounds that occur so often to change the good-looking and previously well-performing acquisition into an ugly duckling are self-inflicted. It is not competition, or economic conditions, or changing technology, that causes the new acquisition to flounder or fail completely. It is the human problems *within* the corporation, specifically between the people of the parent corporate headquarters and those of the previously independent new entity.

It is failure to recognize and minimize those problems that produces the recurring and depressing spectacle of a large corporation announcing only several years after an acquisition that expectations have not been met, management changes have been made, and reorganization and revitalization of the acquired company is being undertaken. A year or two later, divestiture may actually take place.

It is during the first six months to a year of contact between the headquarters people of the parent corporation and the personnel of the acquired entity that the die will be cast. The necessary and, indeed, critical contacts will quickly assume a relationship one way or the other, a relationship that will largely determine whether the acquisition will thrive in its new corporate atmosphere or will lose the qualities that made it interesting to the acquirer in the first place.

Any going business is not a monolithic, one-activity organism but consists of various functions, interrelated but each dealing with activities and problems in its own sphere. Therefore, the following chapters treat the after-acquisition stresses and conflicts that arise in each one of the business areas, for example, finance, personnel and benefits, marketing/sales, technology and manufacturing, public relations.

Each functional area of the business will have its own unique set of problems to face while being integrated into the new corporate parent's world. Though there are general dos and don'ts, the after-acquisition interfacing between the parent headquarters people and those of the acquired entity involve a different set of troublesome situations for marketing from those for finance or the other functions.

Also discussed are the problems and opportunities introduced by the entrepreneurial spirit, as it manifests itself in both the headquarters and the divisions of a corporation. The popular but illusive concept of synergism is examined, since it is frequently considered as the rationale for an acquisition.

The increasing importance of international operations for global markets is recognized by a separate chapter analyzing the differences the international dimension makes in headquarters/line relationships. The normal difficulties are magnified and made worse by the added complexities involved in harmonizing business entities of differing nationalities. These problems are at their worst in an acquisition situation.

Sometimes acquisitions fail simply because the decision to buy was based on premises that are wrong. This is usually because the technological evolution or the markets of the acquired entity are not in the main areas of business activity of the acquiring corporation. Hence they are not well understood by the chief people of the acquirer. In almost every case where this happens, the faulty thinking emanated from the topmost level of the acquiring corporation. Examples are discussed in a chapter on staff and line entrepreneurs.

Other chapters discuss business planning, consultants, and use of corporate staff, all in the context of how to achieve successful integration of an acquired company. A final chapter looks at what happens to entrepreneurs who sell their companies to a larger corporation, and offers advice to acquired personnel: what to do and what not to do after acquisition in order to enhance career prospects in the new environment.

The basic situation assumed is that of a multi-division corporation acquiring a previously independent company engaged in manufacturing and selling products. Still, if an acquisition of a services company is made, for example, one in a financial field, many of the following chapters apply equally well, including those on integrating data processing, international operations, public relations, and personnel and benefits.

My industrial experience has been gained over thirty-five years, including functional expertise in marketing/sales, manufacturing, and engineering followed by twenty years as a division and group general manager. This includes ten years as a vice-president and group general manager of the General Instrument Corporation.

During the general management years I have had the responsibility for integrating nine new or recent acquisitions made by large multi-division corporations. Therefore the chapters are illustrated by specific examples from personal experience, and generally on direct knowledge of staff/line relationships, functional business activities, and the unique problems encountered when trying to integrate acquired companies successfully into a larger, multi-division corporate world.

2

FINANCIAL SYSTEMS AND COMPUTER INTEGRATION

WHEN THE ACQUISITION is legally completed, the usual first step of the corporate chief financial officer will be to send the controller's manual to the new subsidiary's chief financial officer along with a terse note saying, "This is the way we do it. Line up with this. Thanks." Now, it is axiomatic that the corporate chart of accounts of the acquiring company will be different from that of the new subsidiary, so there is immediate disarray in the acquirer's financial troops: "Line up with this?" "How soon?" "Does he have any idea what's involved in making all these changes?"

The second step of the corporate person is usually to send a packet of reporting forms and instructions to the subsidiary's unfortunate financial people. This time the accompanying note says, "This is the way our subs report. Start doing likewise immediately so we can consolidate for top management." The packet of forms and instructions spell out reporting requirements for the new subsidiary that are probably both much more detailed and on a faster time schedule than anything they are currently doing. They view with amazement the headquarters' list, which calls not only for very fast reporting of actual results, with explanations of variances, but also for numerous forecasts: forecast profit and loss and balance sheets, sources and uses of cash, capital expenditures committed and made.

As if this isn't bad enough, as soon as the acquisition is officially completed, the corporate financial headquarters puts the new entity on all its mailing lists, so that every jot and tittle of requests, instructions, admonitions, reprimands, flowing out of headquarters starts hitting the desks of the new financial people.

The receivables expert at headquarters wants a list of all customers whose receivables are over 45 days, whatever the amount, with an explanation by the controller. The headquarters' budget and planning department asks for a detailed restatement of the past three years' P & L and balance sheets, using, of course, the corporate headquarters chart of accounts. The headquarters cost accountant wants an immediate estimate of the effect of higher (or lower) gold prices on the costs.

Now the new financial people are going into shock, and this turns to fear when their chief receives a routine copy of a memo from the headquarters' chief financial officer darkly warning all financial people in the corporation of difficult days ahead (or behind) and ending with the demand, "from the President," that immediate steps be taken to reduce the financial functions expenses and/or personnel by either 5, 7, or 10 percent. (No other numbers are ever used in industry, a remarkable fact that is probably worthy of a dissertation.)

While the acquired company's controller is now rushing frantically back and forth between her office and the general manager's (who has problems of his own), asking what in God's name to do with all this stuff, word comes from the receptionist that three internal auditors have just arrived from headquarters and are even now wandering around scaring the life out of everybody.

After several days these worthies, with stern countenance, announce to the embattled controller that many things being done in the department are not at all in accord with corporate financial policy, beginning with the chart of accounts and running the gamut through the details of forecasting, reporting results, the way cost sheets are made up, the lack of at least three competitive bids on everything purchased, and the inadequacy of the subsidiary's petty cash control. Trying their best to look sad, the internal auditors tell the controller that they must report all this bad news to the corporate chief financial officer and the president. "We hope," they say, "that your answers to our forthcoming report will be able to state that all these problems are corrected."

The new controller now has to have an additional in-basket put on her desk for items from headquarters, which quickly reach the same volume as all her "regular" business, which she used to think represented a full day's work.

Is all this noise, confusion irritation, and frustration necessary? Of course not. Worse, it is destructive. Destructive of the morale of the new subsidiary's financial people. Destructive of establishing good working relationships between the subsidiary and corporate headquarters. Destructive of any feeling of mutual confidence and mutual support, which is difficult to measure but nevertheless an important feature of successful corporations.

The commonsense answer, of course, is simply, "Don't dump all this stuff on the new unit willy-nilly and at once."The planning for, and then execution of, bringing the acquisition's financial systems and financial reporting into line with that of the parent corporation should be done as carefully as the acquisition itself.

How to go about it properly? Very important as a starting point is an immediate summit meeting between the top financial people of corporate headquarters and those of the acquired company. This is best done at the subsidiary itself, to give the headquarters' financial types some direct feel of the new entity. It is also more gracious than a "get yourself into headquarters" notice, which the new division's chief people will be getting all too often in the future anyway. The chief financial officer of the acquirer should preside at this summit, accompanied by the controller, treasurer, and perhaps financial analysis manager, with their opposite numbers of the acquiree completing the gathering.

At the meeting the chief financial officer will explain that he is well aware of all the problems involved in merging or converting the subsidiary's financial systems and reporting to that of the parent; that a schedule of the events that will have to take place, with timetables, will now be worked out between his key people and their opposite numbers in the subsidiary; and that until this is completed and the events/schedules published, no change is to be made in the way the acquired company is doing its financial work. He then describes briefly, or asks his associates to describe, the chief features of the corporation's financial system, the extent and frequency of financial information wanted from subsidiaries, and why it is needed.

Finally, he invites a general discussion of mutually shared problems of all financial functions and assures his hearers he realizes that no financial system is perfect: all are built piece by piece according to the circumstances of a business and the predilections of top management, so that changes that will have to be made in the new entity's accounting practice do not imply technical or moral financial superiority at headquarters.

Indeed he'll be happy to hear and consider any suggestions for improvement in the corporate systems, as the new financial people get acquainted with them.

Now all should be sweetness and light. Cocktails and dinner after the meeting, mutual bonhomie, good fellowship, and reciprocal pledges of support to newfound friends. A happy picture. But, unfortunately, dawn comes and with it the necessity to get on with the transition.

At the detailed planning meetings between opposite numbers, the myriad problems surface quickly enough. The corporate chart of accounts has many more subdivisions of manufacturing expenses than the acquired company uses; the corporate chart of accounts has industrial engineering expenses included in manufacturing, and the new unit has them in engineering; outgoing product freight charges are considered a marketing expense at corporate, while they are in manufacturing expenses at the sub; piece-parts received from its own foreign subsidiaries are booked in simply as material by the acquired company, but the new parent corporation breaks down such internal transfers into material, labor, and overhead, and so on.

The corporate schedule for reporting is almost certainly both faster and more detailed than anything the new division has had experience with. "You mean you want a mid-month forecast of probable changes from the P & L forecast made at the start of the month? But how do we know these numbers until they've happened?" "A telexed weekly cash generation and usage report? Well, OK, but *forecast* cash by weeks? How do we know when the bill for that big capital expenditure will have to be paid? Manufacturing hasn't formally accepted the equipment yet—it's still testing it out."

It quickly becomes apparent, also, that the financial people in the new unit can't make the transition to the new chart of accounts and faster and more detailed reporting by themselves. The other functions will have to be involved: manufacturing, engineering, marketing. So the stew necessarily becomes more complex.

The natural strains between functions in any industrial operation come quickly to the fore. Manufacturing is enthusiastic about the idea of outgoing product freight charges becoming a marketing expense. On the other hand, they see absolutely no merit in shifting industrial engineering expense from engineering to themselves. In some cases, the current organizational lineup will have to be altered, for example, the industrial engineering manager will now report to the manufacturing manager rather than the engineering manager, since his expenses will be in the manufacturing budget. Or should he? Does the organizational lineup have to follow exactly the budget consolidations? It is almost always better that it does.

What about all those subdivisions of manufacturing expense now required by the corporate chart of accounts? Lining up with this from the present classifications goes to the heart of how the acquired company gathers and segregates its cost information. It is certain that changes will have to be made, frequently extensive ones. Cost sheets will have to be rearranged, the methods of overhead allocation reviewed and revised, information taken off of production and quality control records perhaps weekly instead of monthly.

And how about the new, more frequent and more detailed forecasts required? Finance can't forecast intelligently without timely inputs especially from marketing and manufacturing (even though the more experienced and feisty accountants will maintain vigorously that they *can* forecast more accurately, *especially* if they aren't hampered by garbage inputs from the other functions). So marketing and manufacturing must alter their previous way of life. If marketing headquarters at the sub now has to forecast more often and in greater detail, does this spill over into the field? Will the field salespeople now spend more time making out forecast sheets and less visiting customers? Or will the headquarters people do the extra forecasting on their own?

At this point, the general manager of the acquired company has to take a hand, resolving judiciously but firmly and finally the disputed items, not—definitely not—just telling subordinates to "work it out among yourselves." The GM must decide the messy questions and steer the functions in the same direction. He has to support finance's need for additional information provided more often. And, one hopes, he will find reasons why it will help the subsidiary do a better job itself and not just put off the matter by saying, "Well, the new corporate headquarters wants it this way, so we have to do it."

Meanwhile, back at the corporate headquarters, people who do not report to the chief financial officer enter the scene. The corporate director of planning wants to recast the total corporation's financial figures for the past five years to include the new acquisition, and the sooner the better, like next Thursday. The figures required, of course, are in a format different from the new sub's existing historical reports. The marketing director at headquarters wants a flow of information to begin at once, covering backlog levels, current and forecast bookings by product line, price trends, historical data on major customers, etc. The demands continue from the functional directors at headquarters, and each puts new requirements on the subsidiary's financial people.

And here is where the president of the acquiring company must come in. He is sensitive to the requests being made by his functional subordinates. He wants them to have all that information, and on an ongoing basis, because he will need it too, from time to time. So the president doesn't say to the other functions, "Stand back until finance finishes its transition to the corporate chart of accounts and reporting requirements," a procedure that normally should take six months to a year, but he can and should set priorities: the order in which the headquarters' functional requests should be handled at the new division.

This order of priority and degree of urgency will certainly be heavily influenced by the size of the acquired company. If it is so big that a wave in its financial performance could rock the parent's boat, the pressure will be severe to make the necessary changes quickly. Fortunately, the large acquisitions will have a sizeable financial group and probably advanced forecasting reporting systems themselves, so what is required will not be a severe shock to them, and their personnel should be competent to carry through the changes required. If the organization is a small part of the total corporation, more time can be allowed for an orderly changeover, which time will most probably be sorely needed by the small financial group at the sub to whom the new requirements will seem too, too much at first.

To conclude this discussion of financial systems and financial reporting, there are other things the acquirer can do to ease the strain of transition.

First, an interim set of reports can be used for six months to a year. These would provide the basics needed by the parent for consolidations and reports to shareholders, without requiring the full panoply of detail that the parent likes to see and sometimes even uses. Every acquired company will be keeping track of the top and bottom lines of a P & L—sales and after tax income—even if only six lines are used in between compared with, say, 28 of the new parent. All acquired companies will be keeping track of bookings and backlog, a balance sheet will be in existence and maintained reasonably well up-to-date. Those acquired companies whose former president just kept the books on the backs of old envelopes will probably turn out to have a superb grasp of cash flow, more accurate and realistic than many large companies with a full house of accountants. So the basics will be available and can provide what is needed, just given some understanding and forbearance on the part of the acquiring corporation until an orderly transition to the new systems can be made.

Second, there is no eleventh commandment that says all divisions in the corporation, regardless of their size, have to report and forecast in the same level of detail. Why not a sliding scale? The larger the entity and therefore its importance in the consolidated picture, the more detail in its financial reports to headquarters. The small ones to report and forecast in considerably less detail and not every week, not necessarily even every month. A sensible approach, no? And yet it just isn't done. At General Electric, International Telephone and Telegraph and General Instrument, the 10 million dollar sales volume divisions have to report and forecast in exactly the same voluminous detail and on the same time schedule as the 100 million dollar sales volume divisions. This requires disproportionately large financial personnel and expenses in small divisions and adds disproportionately to the burden of their other functions as well. A good place to start with this radical idea would be a small or medium-sized acquisition, thus easing considerably their integration pain.

There should be several follow-up summit meetings during the transition period. At these the top three or four corporate financial people would again sit with their opposite numbers of the new division. Progress in the transition program would be reviewed. Problems requiring high-level resolution would be put on the table. Priorities and time tables would be altered, if appropriate.

The financial function is necessarily one of the most important pieces involved in integrating the acquired company into the larger structure. Applying common sense and recognizing the very real problems presented to the acquiree's financial people can smoothe the transition and establish good will between headquarters and the new acquisition.

Integrating local computer data processing operations into the parent corporation's electronic data processing system presents a thorny problem. Anyone with experience in programming and using computers in business operations knows how complex a matter it is to get systems in place and operating as expected. Then, how even more difficult it is to maintain the systems properly, keep the date bases current, and make changes as desired or needed as business circumstances change.

Computer manufacturers have always glossed over the horrendous complexities of altering a system once in, changing to a larger or smaller computer, buying or producing in-house software programs that are tailored to specific needs, etc. The user's EDP people, however, know only too well the problems involved.

Now add to this picture the desire of large corporations to have fast reporting of divisional financial information to headquarters, to obtain earlier corporation-wide consolidations via a central computer operation. Also the headquarters' desire for instant access to detailed divisional information. Not just financial, you understand, but *everything*: the production level on product x at plant y; the latest quality control reports from manufacturing and customer service; employee turnover ratios; expense account information; the prices on purchasing's latest material requisitions; how much capital expense money has been committed this month; productivity and efficiency ratios in the plants. All this from corporate activities everywhere.

Thus a vast flood of detailed information pours into corporate headquarters. Executives everywhere are coming to require their daily morning "fix" of computer printouts on their desk along with the *Wall Street Journal*.

In theory all this gargantuan effort permits better headquarters "control" over what's going on all over the far-flung corporate empire. Headquarters can "react quickly" to things that are going astray, take "remedial action," order quick zigs or zags to counter changing circumstances.

Does it work? Of course not, but it does produce an illusion of quick action and control and so is much cherished by top management and many other headquarters people. It sounds good for a president to tell security analysts that the corporation's computer system gives instant information on trouble spots anywhere in its empire, allowing the president's equally instant personal intervention to straighten matters out.

What really happens? Let's say line 345 of the morning manufacturing statistics printout shows product line x at plant y producing far below schedule. Let's assume the corporate vice president of manufacturing actually notices this particular item. Alert, he swivels his chair around and, with the computer keyboard next to his desk, calls up on his screen the production level for the line at that plant as of 9:00 A.M. this morning. It shows zero. He immediately orders his secretary to get the plant manager on the phone, but he is out of the office and the secretary leaves a message to call back. "Get him on the phone now!" the vice president roars, "wherever the hell he is." Some minutes later the plant manager calls in. "Where were you," says the VP, "and what's the matter in line x?" "That's where I was," replies the manager, "out on the floor with the people working on it. We're replacing the gizmo valve. It broke. What do you want?" "I want that line up and running as soon as possible," says the vice president. "Well, what the hell do you think we're trying to do?", says the subordinate. "Get off the phone so I can get on with the job." They hang up with neither person's disposition improved for the day's work.

Down the hall at headquarters, the marketing vice president chokes on a gulp of coffee as she notices on line 97 of the morning's statistics printout that bookings for product line a at plant b were zero the previous day, rather than the usual $100,000 more or less. Her secretary can't reach the sales manager for that product line right away because he's on the road visiting customers, so the marketing vice president settles for the supervisor of order service at the plant, who is in no mood for pleasantries. "Of course the printout shows zero for yesterday, and you know why? Because our order entry computer is down, that's why. I've got the customers' orders piling up around my ears, production control is all over me, and now you are on the phone wasting my time." "OK, OK," says the vice president, and quickly hangs up.

This is useful? Well, at lunch that day with the corporate president, the vice president of manufacturing can say that he is on top of the product line x situation, while the vice president of marketing can register a complaint about the reliability of the order entry computers. But meaningful, "quick reaction," "control," etc.? No.

A critical and not yet sufficiently recognized fact is that today in a manufacturing corporation, financial information *is not* the largest user of computer time. Rather, manufacturing information—order entry, production and material control, inventory updating, and marketing/sales information—are the large users. In a manufacturing corporation today, producing the necessary financial reports and consolidations represents only some 25 percent of total computer time, with the other functions, especially manufacturing, requiring 75 percent.

What this means, of course, is that local computing power becomes more and more important while a large central computing operation at or near corporation headquarters becomes more and more an anachronism.

Some giant corporations have recognized this and organized accordingly, but not enough. The myth of central control/immediate headquarters response, so assiduously promoted by large computer manufacturers, dies hard. Even today, most headquarters people still feel obliged to pay lip service to computerized central control. To do otherwise would, after all, diminish the perceived importance of their hands being firmly on the controls.

On a more practical level, there's also the heavy investment in machines and hardware/software systems, many unique to the corporation and the large computers it possesses. Even the stoutest knowledgeable heart quails at the effort and time required to change what is in place.

And there's the rub: stoutest *knowledgeable* hearts. Unfortunately there are stout hearts who launch into enormous computer changeover projects, at great human and financial cost to their own corporations, because they simply do not realize what they are getting into.

A classic example occurred at General Instrument (GI) in the mid-1970s, when there appeared on the scene a new chief financial officer, who set out to install a common chart of accounts across the entire corporation, replacing the existing mosaic of various divisional charts of accounts. A good objective. Overdue at GI, in fact. No problem so far.

However, the program was launched only four months before the end of the fiscal year, with the stern charge to all divisional financial operations to be fully lined up with the new chart of accounts by the beginning of the next year. Then, off with the old. Only use the new chart in making up financial reports.

Rough, since the new chart was considerably more detailed than the one most divisions had been using. Still, achievable if a lot of more important things were brushed aside. The troops were pale but determined, not without legitimate complaint, of course. Like, "Can't we at least discuss the need for all these additional items?" and, "Hadn't we better continue our previous reports in parallel with the new system for a trial period after the new fiscal year starts?" The answers were a blunt "No, quit complaining and get on with the job."

Worse was to come. The central computers/headquarters control system reared its head in truly grandiose form. Every operation in the corporation, not just manufacturing divisions but even sales offices, were to begin the new fiscal year reporting in the format of the entire new chart of accounts, every detail, to the headquarters central computer operation. That already sadly overburdened group would then compute the divisional trial balances and P & Ls and *return* them to the divisions whence the details had come.

The remarkable idea was that headquarters people would be able to scrutinize the divisional financial results at the same time, or even before, division management people saw them. Imagine if you can the kind of totally inane phone conversations that could then ensue. "George, your balance sheet shows you way off forecast on inventory. What's happening?" "Nothing," says George, "Our inputs were wrong. We sent in the corrections, but headquarter's computer people say they're so loaded with other stuff they can't run a new balance sheet for us for 48 hours. If we did the balance sheets here we could correct it now!"

However, before that stage could be reached, the divisions had their hands full reprogramming all their financial information to the new chart of accounts. Because of the short time allowed, in many cases it was necessary to establish a cross-reference table to be able to report to headquarters in the new format while still gathering local financial information in the old format. So, many divisions now had to work with two data bases instead of the desired universal one. Operations outside the United States had to use three, including the one in local currency.

The troops were in disarray now, almost down, rubber-legged but still doggedly punching away, and then came the coup de grace. Two brand new, largest ever, computers were installed in headquarters, replacing the older units whose crochets and foibles were at least known and on which various home-brewed General Instrument software programs had been running for years.

The new computers were supposed to be completely compatible with the old; old software programs would run OK on the new computers. Well, enough of them weren't and didn't so that GI's headquarters computer operations very nearly ground to a halt. Many were the voices then belatedly raised saying, "I could have told you beforehand this whole thing wouldn't work, especially on such a short time cycle," which was a great comfort to the many people in midair frantically making the changeover.

There is a god of corporations, however, who tries hard to save top managements from the worst consequences of many of their own initiatives. In this case the saving circumstance was that almost all divisions were still keeping their own figures in the old way, despite the exhortations to stop. Many of the division general managers and controllers had been around awhile, could show scars to prove it, and had a healthy skepticism toward such mind-boggling changes as had been unleashed by the new chief financial officer on such short notice. Therefore the corporation was able to make consolidations from the division figures, prepared in the old way, until the massive new system got reasonably untangled about six months later.

With this background, let's now look at the EDP problems involved with an acquisition.

The new entity will most probably have a computer, a Honeywell, say. The parent corporation is standardized on IBM (International Business Machines). Of course the headquarters computer people will want to be able to communicate directly with the acquisition's computer. They will also advise the new subsidiary that the corporation is standardized on common programs used by all divisions for general ledger, payroll, receivables, and accounts payable, and that these should be used by the new division.

Concurrently, the acquisition's financial people will be receiving the new common chart of accounts from headquarters finance, new accelerated schedules of reporting, and asking their EDP manager how soon she can make all these changeovers. The beleaguered EDP head considers the enormity of the task ahead, the "as soon as possible" pressure, looks dolefully at her two and one-half programmers, and resigns.

At home that evening, or at a bar, however, she has a stiff drink or two and reconsiders. Surely, she reasons, the managements involved will understand the complexity of the job, the time needed for reprogramming, for trial runs, for developing the new data bases required for the more detailed corporate parent's financial reports.

She returns to the job and proceeds with a good heart—at first. Disillusion sets in when she realizes beyond a shadow of a doubt that most of both managements involved *do not* understand what the EDP people are up against.

Here we reach the nub of the matter. Most corporate presidents, and their chief lieutenants, have a decent working knowledge of what goes on in the basic functional areas of the business: marketing, manufacturing, engineering, personnel, and finance. They have spent time in two or three of the functions on their way up, and their colleagues can fill in each other's gaps. This means a reasonably realistic grasp exists in most top managements of how things are done in the various functions, and what kind of time is required to get changes made.

The exception is computers: electronic data processing. This is terra incognita for many top managements. Sure, they know what computers produce—voluminous printouts of all sorts, some of which they even look at. But time required to produce a new, or change an old program; time required to shift from one computer to another; time required to make two different computers compatible enough to talk to each other; trial runs; correcting program errors; crutching around computer down time—no, most top managements don't have sufficient EDP gauges in their heads to keep their expectations realistic.

This is why there has been so much trouble in industry as computers have become more and more widespread and the siren songs of "central control" and "instant access" have seduced managements into immense cloud nine programs for worldwide computer linkages and instant availability of detailed information.

For an acquisition situation, let's first consider the ideal case. The parent corporation has already in place a good division of EDP work between corporate headquarters and the divisions. The major manufacturing centers have computer hardware on site and handle all their local needs for material control/purchasing, on-line order entry, production scheduling, inventory control, costing, salary and wage computations, etc.

Each division headquarters, wherever located, also has the hardware and software to produce its own financial reports; sales/marketing information; personnel and benefits reports; and customized reports for various levels of management, such as average selling prices vs. last quarter or last year; business planning, and budgeting history and formulas.

With local hardware, the divisions have both the responsibility for and the control of their EDP operations and can respond to problems such as computer down time, make quick corrections to faulty inputs, and modify, add, or eliminate local programs as required by changing circumstances.

Corporate headquarters has a central EDP operation, which receives and processes financial information from the divisional centers for consolidations and headquarters use. The corporate EDP staff also selects from outside software vendors, or produces themselves the kind of programs that can be common throughout the corporation: general ledger, accounts receivable, payroll. The headquarters EDP staff also selects the type of hardware that is used in the divisions, to ensure compatibility and, hopefully, to optimize hardware/software costs.

If the above is the situation in the new parent, then the problems of integrating the new entity into the EDP network are minimized, though certainly not eliminated. Local management will not be asked to give up operational control of their own EDP activity. They will, however, certainly have to change some or many programs, and probably hardware, to reach complete compatibility with a corporate headquarters EDP.

Compatibility means that needed consolidation financial information can be transferred from computer to computer and that the corporation-wide standardized programs can be run on a local computer. To reach compatibility requires time: time for acquiring new hardware, if necessary; time for reprogramming; time for trial runs and error corrections; and finally, time during which the old and new programs are run in parallel to ensure continuity, before pulling the plug on the old programs and hardware.

The immediate crunch arises from corporate headquarters wanting to receive and consolidate the new entity's financial results and forecasts as soon as possible, through the headquarters EDP operation.

This is best done by establishing a cross-reference table between the general ledger and chart of accounts data base of the acquisition and that of the parent corporation. The financial information at the new division continues to be gathered and reported in its normal fashion, and a roll-up or summarization is added using the cross-reference table of the critical numbers needed by headquarters for corporate consolidations. This can be done via computer or manually.

Concurrently, a detailed conversion schedule should be established for revising, installing, and testing the programs necessary to get the division fully onto the new corporate chart of accounts and using the standardized corporate software programs, and to obtain new hardware, including terminals, as required to make the new entity a fully compatible part of the corporation-wide EDP network.

How long should this take? If the situation is normal, that is, if the EDP people, especially programmers, are in short supply and already overloaded, allow 9 to 12 months. If corporate headquarters EDP people, usually overburdened themselves, do happen to be available to work at the division on the changeover, then 6 to 9 months.

Attempts to telescope the time required are continually being made, because of the ignorance factor mentioned earlier, and equally continually produce horrendous snafus. If an impossible schedule for conversion is imposed by fiat, with objections brushed aside by a deadly "you're not being cooperative" attitude on the part of the parent headquarters financial or EDP people, then the real situation goes underground. The new division will *have* to continue their own system to avoid the loss altogether of the ability to generate financial and control reports, while frantically producing numbers for headquarters via a computerized cross-reference table or manual manipulation of local reports.

This only delays obtaining the desired common chart of accounts, common financial reports, and computer hardware and software compatibility across the entire corporation.

So, even where the parent corporation is enlightened and well organized with respect to EDP operations, the better part of a year should be allocated as the time required to change over the new subsidiary to corporate hardware and software compatibility without causing more commotion and waste of valuable people resources than the objective justifies.

At the other end of the efficiency scale is the large corporation whose EDP operations have grown haphazardly, especially where many acquisitions have been made. Here there is no standardization of equipment or corporation-wide use of standard software programs. IBM is used at one place, Honeywell at another, Burroughs at a third. Corporate headquarters has a central EDP operation, of course, but there is little computer transfer of data from divisions to headquarters. Minimal attempt is made by headquarters EDP people to specify and control what equipment and software is used or added to divisional EDP centers. It is laissez-faire to the extreme. But what is not so good for the corporation is fine for the new acquisition. Business as usual in their EDP activity.

In between is the corporation that wants to integrate its EDP activities, use common hardware and software, have computer-to-computer exchange of data, and a headquarters EDP operation that receives and can process information from all over the corporate empire.

However, the integration and standardization is being battled through right now. It is not complete, and headquarters' ideas of what the eventual or ideal EDP arrangement should be may well be changing.

In these circumstances the new acquisition is usually in for a rough time. Clearly, the changes projected or being implemented for the entire corporation should be spelled out from the beginning for the new division. But, also usually, the acquisition finds itself in the forefront of change because of a general "let's start these guys off on the right foot" attitude at headquarters.

Thus the new acquisition is given the ultimate EDP plan perhaps only half-realized throughout the corporation, but presented as being fixed, immutable, and its implementation necessary as soon as possible.

A much better procedure, more efficient as well as more humane, would be to put the acquisition at the bottom of a priority list for divisional changeovers to the ultimate plan. Let the old divisions fight through the trial and error period, the debugging, the parallel operations, the changes of hardware, which software is to be used, what is to be done at headquarters and what at the divisions.

The old line divisions know how to contend with headquarters EDP or finance when their plans and schedules become too unrealistic, or too expensive, or simply unnecessary. They have a track record, a standing in the corporation, friends in vice-presidential seats at headquarters. They can get a fair hearing against too much/too fast dictates from headquarters functions.

The new acquisition has none of these strengths at first. Therefore wise corporate top executives should ensure that in EDP, as in other areas, the new entity is protected by being allowed sufficient time for implementing changes, and by being placed low on the priority list for full EDP integration into the corporate system.

3

PERSONNEL AND
BENEFIT POLICIES

No AREA IN CORPORATE LIFE is more sensitive than employee relations. The attitudes and motivations of employees, the way they perceive the fairness with which they are treated, the whole system of rewarding good performance, making promotions, handling transfers is of basic importance to the health and progress of any corporation that aspires to the top rank. Having a company perceived as a good place to work by prospective local employees, as a promising place to make a satisfactory career by professional people, as reasonable in relations with labor unions, are critical attributes in attracting and holding good people.

Yet this sensitive area is frequently one of the most badly mishandled when acquisitions are made.

Why? Is it because the old saying is true that personnel departments are purposely staffed solely with misanthropes? Is it because the acquiring company doesn't understand the importance of good employee relations? No, it's more complicated than that.

The acquiring company has established personnel policies covering a multitude of things, and usually contained in an employee relations or human resources manual. There will probably be written job descriptions, formal performance evaluations, a salary structure, definite procedures for making salary changes (which ideally bear a close relation to the performance evaluations). There will be a pension plan, a medical insurance plan, a stock purchase plan. There will be rules and regulations on expense accounts, use of company cars, flying coach or first class, perhaps even whether relatives of employees can be hired.

Now, it is always true that the personnel policies and procedures of the newly acquired company will differ from those of the parent corporation, not just in a few particulars, but in many. Some differences will be major, many will be minor, but all are fertile matter for misunderstandings and conflicts.

Therefore it is urgent that the acquirer tread softly in this whole area, considering the impact carefully before mandating changes in the existing panoply of personnel policies at the acquired company. Unfortunately, the acquirer's personnel people at corporate headquarters are eager to change any and all policies and practices at the new subsidiary to make them conform to those at the parent. And they want the changes made *now*. Why the rush? Why do the Dr. Jekylls in corporate personnel so often turn into Mr. Hydes in attacking these matters at a newly acquired company?

The basic rationale cited is the desirability of uniform practice across all parts of the corporation: for reasons of equity, efficiency of administration, facilitating transfers of personnel between corporate units, and so on. These are important considerations, and, indeed, the personnel policies of the acquisition should be brought into uniformity with those of the acquiring corporation—in due course, not hastily by executive fiat from on high as so often happens, creating ill will and hostility toward the corporation among the people at the acquisition.

A good example of how not to proceed was provided by ITT's headquarters benefits people following the acquisition of Cannon Electric. Cannon had been in the ITT fold only 4 months when the headquarters employees benefits director insisted that all Cannon benefit plans be changed to the ITT plans by year-end, only three months away. As the acquisition's newly appointed general manager, I protested vehemently, arguing that doing the job properly and minimizing friction would take at least a year. Though the headquarters man attempted to overcome such opposition by invoking the name of President Harold Geneen—"The boss wants to see the ITT plans in effect everywhere and as soon as possible"—we stuck to, and got, 15 months to make the necessary changeovers.

Now why so long? What is so complicated about this matter? First, general remarks, and then some specifics.

Employee morale tends to be a fragile thing and important to keeping it healthy is employee understanding. The changes in existing policies and procedures that will be necessary must by carefully and fully explained to the people before they are implemented. Sufficient time must then be allowed for a reaction and feedback, and then a second round of detailed explanations and discussions. If thought necessary, then a third round. Overcompensation is vastly preferable here than too little explanation, not enough time for discussion, for feedback, for answering logical questions and quieting emotional or irrational worries.

Comparing two sets of employees relations policies is more complex than it sounds. There will be specific points of more or less importance where the acquiring corporation's policies are somewhat more generous or flexible than the acquired entity policies. You can be sure that the acquired employees will find no difficulty in accepting such changes. On the other hand, there will be, vice versa, points where the acquired company's policies are better from the employees' point of view than those of the new corporate parent. These changes, you can be equally sure, will be viewed with alarm and suspicion by the acquired employees. They will find numerous objections on logical and illogical grounds, possible legal difficulties (they hope), and even lofty moral objections against the offending parts.

All this needs to be sorted through patiently by the headquarters employee relations people and their opposite numbers at the new subsidiary, with the local general manager's full participation. To make the transition as smoothly as possible, the GM must understand the necessary changes in detail in order to participate actively in explaining and defending the new policies. All key managers, not just the personnel people, must know the trade-offs, that is, the places where the old policies are somewhat better than the new ones, and where the new ones are better. Obviously, the head executive at the acquisition should not take the limp position, "Well, this is the way it is with the new parent corporation, so that's it."

Everyone knows the old line, "There's no reason for it, it's just our policy." In order to minimize the objections and worries about changes in the existing policies and procedures, the acquirer's headquarters people must discuss fully the reasons behind the corporation's policies and procedures.

Sometimes, of course, business philosophy is involved. It is not necessary that all of the newly acquired employees agree with the philosophy behind the policies, but they should understand what they are. This is an important part of integrating new employees into the larger corporation and helping them to become effective contributors to it.

Let's consider salary structure and salary administration, a subject of great interest at all times. The acquiring corporation most probably has a formalized salary scale with all jobs: labor, clerical, professional, ranked in order from the lowest—sweeper perhaps—to the highest—president or chairman of the board. Each position has a pay or salary level attached to it with minimum and maximum amounts allowable for that particular job level, perhaps varying by location. Each employee in the theoretically perfectly administered corporation is being paid somewhere in his or her range, with the exact position determined by performance. Now, of course, especially in a large corporation there will be anomalies, for a whole host of past or current reasons. Here and there an employee will be being paid above the maximum, other employees below the minimum of their job level. But there will be a formal structure in place.

Similarly in the acquired company, but now complications arise because the two structures do not match. In the parent corporation, division marketing and engineering managers are equal, and a level higher than manufacturing managers. At the acquiree the VP of engineering has top salary among the functional managers; there are even some companies where the controller is highest paid. And these differences extend right down through the organization chart. Field sales managers rate higher than quality control managers at the acquirer, lower at the acquiree. Design engineers are rated higher than manufacturing supervisors on the acquirer's chart; they are rated equal on the acquiree's chart.

Beyond these differences are thornier problems. When an employee is promoted to a higher level, is there an immediate salary increase or is this delayed for six months, say, to see how the person handles the new responsibilities? Or does it occur on the regular anniversary date of the last increase?

What about tenure—length of time on the job? Should an employee get some increase every year, even if the maximum salary of that position has been reached? Or is some promotion necessary to move on up in salary? Is the 40-year-old laboratory technician with a wife and three children really going to be paid exactly the same as the 25-year-old with no family responsibilities who is doing the same job? Since salaries move up with better performance, should they be adjusted downward if poor performance occurs at a later date? All good, debatable questions.

The position of an employee within a salary range is determined by performance, or it should be. Well, how is performance measured? At the corporation, besides the job description, there is required each year a specific set of goals to be accomplished, which are checked over at salary review time. The acquired company has job descriptions but believes that an individual's performance each year is affected by so many things outside the employee's direct control that only a subjective evaluation of quality of performance by the bosses is possible.

Is an inflation factor used, and if so, how is it handled? The acquired company has been adjusting its levels each year automatically by whatever inflation rate the government announces. The new parent does not.

Now the stage is set. The corporate salary administration people meet with their counterparts at the new subsidiary and begin to review and discuss these matters. Since there is no subject more important to most employees, including these salary administrators, and since many of the issues are emotional or subjective ones, and certainly debatable, the level of discussion becomes quickly intense. There are no other subjects on which such divergent—and strongly held—opinions exist.

Someone who believes that an older employee should be paid more than a young one, even if they are doing the same job, is simply not going to be converted by the arguments of the person (perhaps a young one) who firmly believes that age should not be a factor in salary evaluations. The executive who believes that a pay increase should accompany any promotion, since larger responsibilities are immediately being handled, and as a vote of confidence, is not going to be converted because some other executive argues vehemently that the newly promoted employee must succeed in the new job before being so rewarded.

Even though desirable, it is not possible in these matters that the newly acquired people agree completely with the corporate policies on salary administration. In any group of executives there will never be unanimity on this subject. But the past policies must be explained and defended again and again to ensure at least understanding before the new sub's salary administration is brought into line with the parent.

How is this transition best made? First of all, it should be recognized at once that the process will require the longest time span of all activities requiring integration into the parent. Two to three years is about minimum. Five may be better. Fortunately, although it is extremely important to individuals, there is not the same time urgency about this as, for example, about a company's getting the financial statements lined up with the parent's, so sufficient time can be taken.

The fact that anomalies do exist already here and there in the parent corporation helps understanding on the headquarters side. The HQ salary administrators already are living with situations that are out of policy limits. The new acquisition brings with it a lot more, but the treatment is the same. Make the necessary adjustments over several years so as not to affect drastically any employee all at once.

If there are compelling reasons for leaving certain situations as they are, don't insist on changes just for uniformity's sake. There will always be some anomalies, especially the larger the corporation, no matter how disciplined salary administration is in general. So given time, patience, sufficient consideration of unusual circumstances, and working at it, three to five years after the acquisition, the acquired company will be as much in line with corporate salary administration as any of the older divisions.

The sensitive and emotional issue of salary administration and its importance is well illustrated by the fact that the top executives of acquiring companies almost always tread carefully in this area. In any other matter, the tendency of the acquirer's president is to issue quick instructions for full integration into the corporate structure as soon as possible—a kind of "damn the torpedos, full speed ahead" approach. But not in salary administration, and rightly so. The acquired company is successful because of its people, and a big factor in their morale is the belief that they are being treated fairly in what the corporation puts in their paycheck.

In the area of benefit plans, pension and medical insurance are the most important. Not nearly as highly charged an issue as salary administration, still pension and insurance matters raise a lot of hackles when changes are necessary.

Well, you are completely familiar with the pattern by now. There are differences between the acquirer's plans and acquiree's plans. The employees at the new subsidiary will worry that the existing benefits may be reduced. The acquirer will be torn between wanting to make the necessary changes ASAP (as soon as possible) and the desire to establish good rapport and confidence between the corporation and its new subsidiary.

What are the pension differences? Amount, of course, and how it is calculated. Then, vesting, because today fewer and fewer people spend all their career with one company. So younger employees as well as older are interested in a pension plan's vesting provisions, as well as its amount. Can an employee continue to be covered under the company's group insurance plan after retirement?

The medical benefit plan is increasingly important as hospitalization costs and surgeons' fees keep mounting. Does one plan have a dental care provision and not the other? How do the maternity benefits compare for female employees? How are the benefits for dependents of employees?

Direct experience with some 25 or 30 benefits plans shows that despite the various differences, they will almost always be a standoff. After all, industry lives in a competitive world. Just as in salary levels, a company, large or small, has to be reasonably competitive in pension and medical benefit plans or they won't attract and then hold the good people.

Even so, the various differences between the acquirer's plans and those of the new subsidiary need careful sorting through. Point-by-point comparison should be made and then discussed in a detailed write-up, which should be distributed to all employees. Chart-illustrated presentations and question-and-answer round tables should be held with small groups of employees. The ordinary worriers should be reassured as much as possible, while the people who want to complain endlessly about any unfavorable differences should be treated with more patience than they deserve.

Most large corporations do not have a profit-sharing plan where some part of the total pretax income is divided up among all employees. Rather, various incentive or bonus plans are used in the divisions of the corporation where they can be closely related to the performance of that particular division. An acquired company, the equivalent of a division of the acquiring corporation, may well have a profit-sharing plan. What to do about that? Clearly, a large corporation cannot have profit-sharing plans in some of its divisions and not all. So how do you handle the elimination of a profit-sharing plan at the sub?

Two newly acquired companies in the General Instrument group for which I was responsible had come in with profit sharing plans. The C. P. Clare Company plan allocated a share of pretax profit to a fund, each employee's portion of which was determined by salary level. However, the funds were not distributed each year; rather, the accumulated amount was turned over to each employee upon retirement or leaving the company. The "whenever you leave" provision was bad because good people had been lost from time to time, just to get their accumulated funds.

Since the profit-sharing plan funds were intended for retirement use, Clare has no regular pension plan. So the idea that suggested itself was to replace profit sharing with a standard pension plan. On the surface, this doesn't sound very attractive: profit sharing has a good press. But regular company contributions to a pension plan, in bad years as well as good, do protect employees from the vicissitudes of bad business years.

Clare management people were divided over the proposal, those against predicting mass defections of good people and a sullen remaining group if we eliminated profit sharing. Those for the change, however, pointed out that Clare had just completed two poor financial years, in which the earnings had been so small that the contribution to the profit-sharing plan was minimal, and also that having a more standard pension plan would eliminate the problem of good people leaving from time to time to get their accumulated profit-sharing funds.

Final consensus for making the change was achieved by considering what was to be done with the existing funds in the profit-sharing plan. They couldn't just be rolled over into the GI plan because of legal restrictions. So the proposal included immediate distribution of the accumulated individual shares as soon as the new pension plan was installed. No employee had to leave Clare in order to get the accumulated money—have cake and eat it too. As a final fillip, for any employees who chose, we offered to keep their accumulated shares in an interest-earning fund, to be finally paid out on retirement or whenever they left the company. The employees chose overwhelmingly to take their money now. The profit-sharing plan was discontinued and the GI pension plan was installed.

At Chicago Miniature Lamp Company (CML) there also was no pension plan, but the profit-sharing money was distributed each year—bird in hand. The opening for a reasonable changeover did exist, however, in that the existing salaries at CML were well below General Instrument levels. Following due consideration and debate, a three-year program was established to raise salaries to the GI level while concurrently scaling down the profit-sharing distribution each year, until it was eliminated in the fourth year. Then, when the GI pension plan was installed, we credited years of past service. Where there has been a profit-sharing plan, most professional employee relations people don't like to recognize in addition past service in the new plan, feeling that it represents "double payment," as it were. In this case, we believed it fair in the overall balance to do so.

There remains one other area in benefits, that is, fringe benefits or perquisites, which, while not as basically important as salary administration, pension, or medical insurance, nevertheless loom large in a company's image. Here the variations are tremendous, primarily simply as a result of the chief executive's personal feelings about such things. One president thinks a good bash should be thrown once in a while because "all work and no play makes a dull executive." Another believes any such blow-out will threaten to unravel the well-disciplined work ethic of key employees, and so on.

The extremes are well illustrated by ITT and General Instrument. At ITT one can expect to enjoy lavish parties to which wives and husbands are invited. Executive seminars are held at the world's finest resorts, with distinguished guest speakers, evening entertainment ranging from the local symphony orchestra to Art Buchwald, and plenty of swim or golf time. The most sumptuous of these affairs is held every three or four years at Boca Raton.

First class air travel is always used by the upper echelons. Company cars are plentiful, chauffeured at New York headquarters and the larger European subsidiaries, self-driven by the semideprived.

ITT managers had to work hard, and they took a lot of abuse at planning and operations review meetings, but none could complain about the extracurricular perquisites they enjoyed.

General Instrument? On executive fringe perks we move sharply from the sublime to the ridiculous. Managerial seminars are held in spartan locations and are strictly business. Business sessions are held all day and after dinner each evening. Not one afternoon is set aside for socializing. Wives and husbands of executive personnel are basically ignored. Company cars are grudgingly provided for salespeople only, with type of car and mileage allowance limitations that would tax Job's patience. Air travel is never first class.

However, the question is, What is the practical effect of such different life-styles? Can you relate corporate performance to the presence or lack of such managerial fringes? No. How important is the ITT approach vs. General Instrument's in morale of key people? Very difficult to say because of the many other factors involved.

For example, all of General Instrument's key executives have made very large capital gains since 1978 on stock options because GI's common has gone up 600 percent in the past five years. This kind of bonanza is obviously more meaningful than a dearth of hail-fellow-well-met affairs, or even having to travel tourist class regularly from New York to Taiwan.

Where the acquired company has been an austere one and the acquirer has more perks, the transition to a higher standard of living seldom causes difficulty.

But if the acquired company has more executive perks than the new parent, what then? A fine example is Bank of America's acquisition of the Charles Schwab brokerage house in 1982. At Schwab, the executive performers can have any automobile they want, leased for them by the company. Not too surprisingly their parking lots are full of Mercedes, Volvos, BMWs. Bank of America, on the other hand, has a rather skimpy automobile policy, with their executive cars running heavily to Buicks and Oldsmobiles.

Bank of America's planning vice president did not notice this particular wrinkle when considering the acquisition, but he is surely aware of it now since, within a large corporation, all roads intersect in the area of employee benefits, including managerial perquisites. The planning vice president has stated that no change in automobile policy is under consideration, either at Bank of America or at Schwab, and that no particular action is called for in a hurry. Wise! The acquiring corporation should tread slowly and warily in such a situation. Certainly not order a drastic reduction in the standard of living of the acquired people. Not without considerable soul-searching and preparation.

Still, in the end, no large corporation can permit large differences in the perks given executives in its various operations to continue indefinitely. There is the general idea of equity, of justice, of ability to transfer executives from one area to another, of obtaining good people to agree to work in the less favored operations, all militating against widely differing managerial perks within one corporation. The differences between the new acquisition and its parent's benefits will have to be minimized, and eventually eliminated.

What will be the resolution in the Bank of America/Schwab case? My money is on the side of the buyer, the HQ people. Sooner or later the automobile policies will be brought into line. Either Bank of America executives will start to drive BMWs, or we will begin to see Oldsmobiles in the Schwab lot.

4

MARKETING/SALES
INTERFACES

MUCH AS ENGINEERS and financial people dislike to acknowledge it, marketing/sales is the cutting edge of any business. Success or failure over the long run depends on a flow of orders from customers for products. Therefore, marketing/sales inputs to the basic questions facing a manufacturing business are crucial, decisive factors.

What products will sell; what features and modifications they must have; what prices are obtainable; on what terms and conditions; what competitors are doing; the acceptance of their products or lack of it by your targeted customers; changes of critical personnel in customers' operations—new purchasing people, new engineers, new quality control experts, and who among the young comers in their organizations will be the critical future influences on buying decisions. Therefore, the heads of any manufacturing company are very sensitive to every vibration coming along the sales antennae.

Also, in sales and marketing, unlike other functions, where the integration problems are solely between the new parent and the acquiree, there are two additional unpredictable and arbitrary players, that is, customers and competitors.

Customers will not at first take much notice of an acquisition. They are busy with many problems of their own and don't really care about the new ownership unless it threatens to upset existing lines of communication and supply. And there is the rub. At the announcement of an acquisition, tremors go all along the network of existing lines of communication between suppliers, sales people, distributors, representatives, and customers.

A distributor who has been a good sales channel for the acquired company but handles a competing product line against another division of the large acquiring corporation will fear that the new parent will order the acquired entity to drop him. He places phone calls in all directions: to the acquired company seeking reassurance that no changes will be made just because of the new owner; he will call other distributors regarding policies and practices of the new owner; he will call other manufacturers of the "threatened" product line to determine if he can pick up their product to replace the existing one if necessary. The largest or brassiest distributors will even contact the acquirer's corporate headquarters, demanding immediate assurances that no changes will be made, with the ink still drying on the acquisition agreement. Representatives will be doing the same.

The formerly independent company's sales offices will be abuzz with rumors: the corporate parent intends to eliminate the new subsidiary's own sales offices and sell the products through their own, to save money; at least the existing sales offices will be merged with other corporate offices, eliminating salespeople; the field sales offices will no longer report to their existing boss but instead will now report to someone or other at the new corporate headquarters; there will no longer be any sales bonus plan; salespeople will have to pay for their own cars.

Rumors will also abound at the acquirer's other divisions' sales offices. These will have a "let's get ours" content: we are going to add the new entity's products to our existing lines, getting more sales; or, we will become responsible for their sales offices, enlarging our empire; there will be a realignment of sales regions and districts of the entire corporation, creating additional high-level sales jobs. Some among the acquirer's salespeople will not scruple at attempting to make their favorite rumors become a reality by lobbying intensively with corporate headquarters people, and by contacting their opposite numbers at the acquired company to inform them that the desired changes *will* be taking place—soon. These contacts, of course, produce predictable results at the acquiree: still more rumors, confusion and fear among the faint-hearted, irritation among the stout-hearted.

Now enter competitors. Always glad to lend a helping hand, these stalwarts with widely varying degrees of imagination and subtlety, will offer to more or less willing ears among the customers the most remarkable explanations and predictions concerning the acquisition and what will follow from it in terms of what the customers can expect from the new corporate marriage—all bad of course.

It is to minimize the confusion and damage from this kind of furor, which will undoubtedly take place—and quickly—following an acquisition, that very early and specific policy decisions and announcements should be made by both the coporate parent and the new entity. Internally to the marketing/sales organizations of both the parent and the new division. Externally: to representatives, distributors and customers.

Since the acquisition was not made in a vacuum, or overnight, but rather studied at some length before hands were shaken on a deal, the marketing vice president at the acquirer's headquarters already knows what the acquirees products, customers, and channels of distribution are, probably having been one of the important voices urging that the acquisition be made. The VP knows where the overlaps are in sales/distribution systems and has already given some thought to minimizing problems and conflicts and integrating the new entity into the existing corporate marketing/sales policies and practices. The vice president must be prepared to issue very soon, along with the acquiree's head marketing person, specific announcements to the fields sales offices, both for their benefit and for transmittal to customers.

If the different product divisions of the parent corporation have their own sales organizations, which is most common, the announcement should state that this is the way Omega Corporation operates, and the new Alpha division will continue to operate its individual sales activities. If, as occasionally, somewhat similar products are grouped together and sold through a common sales organization, the announcement should so state, distasteful as it will be to Alpha division, and it should say which of the existing corporate sales organizations Alpha will participate in. If, rarest of all but a constant temptation to headquarters people, the corporate marketing vice president actually attempts to manage all the sales activities in the corporation, the announcement should boldly say so, even though it cannot be made intelligible how such a gargantuan job could actually be done by any one person.

Though the early and specific announcements will not please everyone, they will remove uncertainty and help turn attention back to the basic job of the sales organizations: selling.

Dealing with the existing representatives/distributors network necessarily is more complex and will have to take longer. These sales channels are independent business people who are selling Alpha's products because it is good business for them today, but they have no long-term tie to the supplier of the salary or career strength, as an employee of Alpha has. Also, they all have been whipsawed from time to time by various manufacturers who let them work hard to build up business in an area and then announce that the product line is being taken away, either given to another rep or distributor, or handled directly by an Alpha sales office. Therefore, these organizations will be extremely suspicious of what may happen, and with good reason.

Now, unlike the rapid disposition of the matter of structure and control of internal organizations in Omega Corporation, the representatives/distributors matter cannot be determined in advance. It must be addressed after the acquisition is completed, because the steps that must be taken in order to decide involve too great a disclosure of the impending acquisition.

The structure of representatives and distributors both at existing Omega divisions and at the newly acquired entity must be reviewed and discussed in detail, *both* with the new division *and* with the representatives and distributors involved. Where are the overlaps? Which representatives and distributors are handling product lines competitive with other corporate divisions' products? Where this is the case, how important are those particular channels to Alpha division? Should the "no competitors" rule be enforced absolutely without exception? Should it be enforced at once, or after, say, six months or a year? How good are the Alpha distribution channels compared with those being used by other divisions of the corporation? In some areas Alpha could be helped by changing to a strong distributor already handling other corporate products and willing to take on more. In some cases the reverse may be true; Alpha's distributor is the best available, and other Omega divisions could benefit if he would agree to handle their lines. A representative in one area may have a special "in" with buyers or engineers of a large customer, perhaps based on expert product and application knowledge, perhaps because he is the customer company president's son-in-law.

All these considerations should be thrashed out in detail between the parent corporation, the new division, and the affected representatives and distributors. The common mistake at the acquirer's headquarters is to make unilateral decisions too soon, based on insufficient information. The existing distributors and representatives of the acquired company should a fortiori have their day in court, in personal discussions and in writing. Technical expertise, past performance, and future plans can all be put in writing. The in-law type of customer connection seldom appears in print, but it can be said in private.

After several months, preferably no longer, because sales effort definitely suffers during this period, the representatives/distributors situation must be straightened out in an optimum way given the specific circumstances. There will be some losers, some hard feelings, some perhaps long-standing connections that will have to be severed. On the other hand, the better distributors and reps will be reassured and perhaps made stronger by additional product lines from other divisions of the acquiring corporation. However it ends up, the basically careful and fair approach used by the corporate headquarters people will go a long way toward avoiding creating lasting problems, both within and outside the corporation.

Even during the short period of several months involved to make these determinations, this area will represent a moving target: distributor A retires; representative B drops your lines for those of a competitor; distributor C's best salesperson leaves to join another company; representative D dies.

Moving on from early decisions and announcements that should be made with respect to field sales channels—direct, representative, and distributor—let's now consider the range of corporate/division interfaces necessary for the long haul, and how to make them effective rather than troublesome.

The new parent corporation will have a marketing vice president or equivalent and staff, who will be struggling courageously to impose a kind of overall order on the essentially chaotic and fast-moving marketing/sales situations throughout the corporation.

The responsibilities of the headquarters marketing people are basically twofold: first and foremost, determining, then reviewing and re-reviewing, what businesses the corporation should be in, that is, what industries and specific customers should be concentrated on, what kind of products and services should be offered; and second, what is the degree of marketing/sales expertise and professionalism present in the various divisions and how effectively are the marketing/sales activities being carried on?

The divisions' responsibilities are to pursue single-mindedly the promotion and sale of its product range; to give key customers the attention they deserve; to get good prices; to recommend additions to and deletions from the product line; to forecast volume and pricing changes; to anticipate competitors' moves.

The divisions' sales/marketing people are in the middle of the battle, in the front-line no-man's-land between customers and competitors. They are busy! At headquarters people are not in among the trees. They can see the forest, can take a more detached, objective, view. Further, they are *expected* to critique the division's personnel and performance.

Given all this, the multiple opportunities for problems and misunderstandings damaging to the overall corporate welfare are easy to see.

As so often in the integration process, the top headquarters person in the function, the marketing vice president, must take the lead in recognizing the danger areas and getting a new relationship off to a good start by minimizing the conflicts.

Does the corporation have product line managers at marketing headquarters, whose job is to provide knowledgeable two-way communication between divisions and headquarters? If so, bring in someone from the acquired company for that job. This will foster confidence among the acquired entity's people.

ITT used to provide classic examples of how not to do it: for example, when the Sheraton Hotel chain was acquired by ITT, the executive vice president of the *Hilton* chain was hired as headquarters product line manager for hotels! Instant conflict, with predictable problems of an adversary relationship from the start.

Does the corporation have area sales people rather than product line sales? Does it have industry rather than product or other sales concentration? Does it have combined sales offices, that is, offices handling a number of divisions' products, or the manager reporting to someone in corporate headquarters?

No fast decisions are necessary in considering and resolving the myriad of philosophical and operating items involved in these matters. It is important for the acquirer to keep clearly in mind that the new company has been, and is, successfully in business: yesterday, today, and probably tomorrow, if *no* changes are made.

As always, the temptation is great at headquarters to *make* changes, to tinker with the acquired entity, to force conversion to its brand of orthodoxy, to achieve instant acceptance of cherished headquarters dogmas as absolute verities.

The very real problems that can arise when the acquirer makes quick changes in a new division's marketing/sales approach were illustrated when ITT acquired General Controls. This company was a vest-pocket edition of Honeywell's temperature control activity, making thermostats of all sizes and shapes, including a large proportion of customized items for important industrial customers. General Control's field sales effort was powered by its own, full-time, on-the-payroll sales engineers. The ITT group general manager to whom the new entity reported, however, had come from an industry where sales were usually handled through representatives, independent business people, rather than by salespeople on a divisions's payroll.

The advantage of using representatives is that they get paid only when sales are made, so that field sales expenses vary directly with sales volume. This contrasts with maintaining one's own field sales force, which represents a continuing level of expense, regardless of sales volume. On the other hand, an on-the-payroll sales force is completely dedicated to selling just your own products, whereas the independent representative may be handling a dozen or more product lines. It is concentration of effort, usually by more effective and technically competent salespeople because of single-minded attention to one product line, versus automatically reduced sales expenses when volume is slack.

This example is not to argue that, all things considered, a 100 percent own sales force is better than representatives, or that reps are better. It is to illustrate what happens when sweeping changes are made too quickly in a business's sales approach. In the General Controls situation, the ITT group general manager decreed that the field sales force should be disbanded and replaced by a network of independent sales representatives. This was done, and the effect the ITT manager was looking for was realized. Sales expenses dropped dramatically. But even as he was taking bows for this achievement, the *unintended* effect became painfully evident: sales of General Control's products also dropped dramatically. Previously smoothly working customer contacts and relationships were disrupted by the rapid disappearance of previously well-known salespeople. Their replacement by reps, who, even with the best of intentions, could not fill the gap quickly, opened the doors to competitors who proceeded to capitalize on General Controls disarray in the marketplace. The reduction in sales expense came nowhere near offsetting the loss of business, and the denouement was that it required five years before General Controls again reached its previous level of market penetration.

How does the corporate headquarters go about fulfilling its responsibility to evaluate the effectiveness of the acquisition's marketing/sales effort? The prerequisite is that the people on HQ marketing staff be capable of making such an evaluation. They must be broad-minded enough to understand and tolerate a diversity of sales approaches used by the corporation's divisions. The customer focus utilized by a division selling an industrial product to engineers will be quite different from one selling a consumer product through supermarkets. The importance to a division of customized products as compared with standard types will vary.

Approaching this task with a new acquisition requires more tact than with a division long within the corporation. The key to minimizing the inevitable resulting friction is for the HQ people to keep an open mind. Whatever the acquisition is currently doing in its marketing/sales activity can't be all wrong. If it was, the acquirer would not have been interested in the first place. Therefore patience is in order while the staff people learn why the new entity handles marketing and sales matters the way they do.

Does the acquired company use mostly representatives for field sales, except that in Seattle there is a company office with full-time salespeople on the payroll? To someone at headquarters used to thinking of Los Angeles and San Francisco as the prime sales areas on the West Coast, this may seem strange, until he finds that the Boeing Company is the largest customer for the acquisition's line of lighted push-button switches for aircraft cockpit and cabin applications.

The headquarters staff person used to regular new product introductions that supercede earlier designs every four or five years looks askance at first at the acquisition keeping in its catalog a product fifteen years old. Then she learns that just one customer, Westinghouse, represents a substantial volume of ongoing business for that old design. Westinghouse needs it as replacement parts for older industrial control systems that are still in use.

When the C. P. Clare Company was acquired by General Instrument, its marketing people had to spend several years explaining to GI headquarters that the relays being manufactured were indeed needed by telecommunications equipment companies, and would be for many more years to come. HQ doubts about the viability of relay products arose out of a common misperception. Because many advanced communication systems being developed in laboratories and by design engineering groups eliminated relays entirely, HQ leaped to the conclusion that the going relay business was in danger of imminent demise. What was lacking was the realization that an advanced communications switching system being developed today in a laboratory is probably two or three years from initial production, and five years from volume production. Then, even after the no-relays switching equipment is in full flight, the more numerous systems that do use relays will still be produced, and for a long time.

Of course, though there is always a reason why the acquired company is handling sales a certain way, the originally good reason may have been invalidated by later events. In examining sales results in the different regions of the country, the headquarters staff person notes that the southeastern region, handled by a representative, seems definitely below the other regions in productivity, even though the customer list is just as extensive. Discussion develops the nature of the problem. The current representative is a son of the original rep, who was a friend of the entrepreneur who founded the acquired company. Though the father had done a good sales job in the past, the son was not pulling his weight in the present. Because of the past close relationship between company and rep, however, the acquisition's salespeople had been reluctant to insist on better performance by the son.

Or a certain product is limping along with low and declining sales, and a poor cost-price relationship in addition. It turns out, that the product was a pet idea of the company's founder that just didn't turn into a success. Yet out of deference to the founding entrepreneur, who may well be no longer on the scene, the acquisition's marketing people have been reluctant to eliminate that item from their market basket.

The HQ people have the duty to put such situations in perspective for the acquisition's marketing group and gently but firmly insist on corrective action. The "gently" is appropriate because such matters are seldom of life-and-death importance. Action does not have to be precipitate. Time can be allowed for consideration of worries or possible problems as seen by the new division's salespeople.

What is needed is a deliberate sorting out of all the marketing/sales activities at the acquisition by the headquarters marketing people and their opposite numbers in the new division, this work to be headed and monitored by the corporate marketing vice president and the equivalent person at the division. The final decisions should not be left to headquarters subordinates. Only the top corporate marketing person should be empowered to say what *must* be changed in the new entity's marketing operations, and what can be left alone.

As in all other functional areas, the acquired entity won't appreciate all this attention: new people involved, with new ideas; existing market/product orientations and biases being challenged by the frequently less than tactful types from headquarters.

However, this is an area where the headquarters people must have early and complete disclosure. The new entity will have to put on the table all their facts and figures with respect to customer ranking; with respect to competitors' relative positions, the acquisition's marketing people's view of what is going on, and what is being done to tilt customers more toward their product offerings; and in order to foil the competitive bad guys and to grow and prosper.

Certainly before the acquisition was made the top people at the parent, including marketing and business planning vice presidents, considered market and product synergism, if any; the general reputation in the trade of the potential acquisition; the degree of customer overlap or conflict. Overlap in the sense of complementary product lines for the same customer: the parent may make computers and the new acquisition makes power supplies for computers. Conflict in the sense that if the parent supplies electronic components to manufacturers of telephone switching systems, then it will want to weigh the pros and cons carefully before acquiring a manufacturer of switching systems, thus putting itself into competition with important customers.

Even with the preparatory work, however, the acquirer cannot know all the facts and figures in advance. Thus, its headquarters marketing people must dig in very soon to learn the real current and expected situation, and to identify potential problem areas, so something can, it is hoped, be done about them before they cause problems with customers and happiness among competitors.

The acquirer will want right away a list of customers, with sales and bookings history for several years back. This scares the wits out of the new subsidiary's people, because such information would obviously be extremely valuable to competitors. It is closely held in the new subsidiary, and their fear is that, once out of their hands and floating around God knows where in the corporate headquarters recesses, it will somehow get to competition.

Even worse is the headquarters request for specific product prices to go along with the customers' sales/order information. Fear of disclosure redoubles, of course. The new entity tries to stave off further digging by producing catalogs with list prices and, perhaps, quantity discounts, but if the situation is normal, a lot of business, especially for customized products, is being done at prices that are worked up for specific quotations. So the headquarters people ask to see whatever pricing rules are in place and used to develop prices for specific quotes.

Well, no one likes to say, "We do it by the seat of our pants," or "We charge whatever the traffic will bear," even though that is very often the case. Those statements really mean the same thing: that the pricing people consider the cost of the product, the customer history, the competitive situation, their backlog and production status, and then comtemplate their navels until inspiration strikes.

Because pricing usually is simply not done on any consistent basis that will bear scrutiny by the scientifically minded, and because most people hate to admit it, the headquarters people invariably have to wade through a remarkable amount of nonsense before obtaining intelligible pricing information.

In evaluating the effectiveness of a new acquisition's sales activities, the headquarters people should be careful about going to outside sources for information, especially to distributors, representatives, and customers.

A favorite technique of ITT HQ marketing used to be to go directly to an acquisition's distributors and ask them whether there were any problems with the new division that ITT headquarters ought to know about. An all but irresistible temptation for the distributor, or course. He would roll out his favorite list of grievances and expound on them at great length. Yes, prices are too high; shipments too slow; quality problems abound; competitors are bringing out better new designs. He would paint an altogether dismal picture for the attentive HQ staff person.

The only question that seemed never to occur to the HQ visitor to ask was, If this division's general situation is as bad as you portray it, how come you bother to handle their products? The distributor was selling the products because the overall pluses outweighed the minuses, of course. But the HQ person asked about problems and so heard a lot of them. Thus armed, the staff expert would then attack the division people at the next review meeting, informing them that he knew from their own distributors what a terrible reputation they had acquired in their business.

This approach helps a corporate headquarters achieve good rapport with its divisions, including acquisitions? Obviously not. When a HQ marketing person wants to talk directly with a division's representatives or distributors, he should be accompanied by someone from the division.

This enables HQ to hear both sides of the story at once if there are differences of opinion on product and performance. It also shows the distributor that corporate HQ doesn't intend to let itself be maneuvered into interfering in normal business relationships between a division and its field sales representatives.

Even more risky is a multi-division corporate HQ visiting customers to inquire about degree of satisfaction with its various divisions' products and services. If the HQ person is the president or a vice president, protocol demands that he or she be received by the customer's top executive or one just below the top.

Usually the executive visited will not be right on top of the situation. "The president of Omega Corp. is coming to see me Wednesday. What the hell does she want?" he asks the purchasing agent. "She wants to know how happy or unhappy we are with her Alpha division. That's the old Camden Company, which Omega acquired recently," the PA replies. "Oh, the outfit that makes the instrument panels we use," says the president. "Well, are we happy?" "Their prices could be better," naturally says the PA. "OK, talk to the engineers and the manufacturing people. They are sure to have some beefs we can use on her. Maybe we can get a price reduction."

The Omega president duly arrives, gets an earful, and departs. It is to be hoped she doesn't get carried away and make a grand gesture, such as agreeing to lower prices. Back home at the head office she mobilizes various staff aides to check into the customer's complaints, which in turn creates extra work at the instrument panel division: explaining, defending, counterattacking. A worthwhile exercise for the chief executive of a large, multi-division corporation? Perhaps, but if so, only indirectly, in the sense that listening to customers' complaints does tend to keep a person's feet on the ground.

It does frequently happen that the newly appointed chief executive of a large corporation announces plans to spend time visiting customers in order to learn directly how they feel about the divisions' efforts to gain their business. This seemingly laudable impulse lasts about six months, a year at most. It loses out to a host of other, more pressing matters that the top person must attend to at the home office. Also, it quickly becomes apparent to the chief executive that the customers are not going to give unbiased opinions and that the divisions' salespeople and general managers are closer to the scene and therefore better equipped to deal with the items discussed.

We are speaking of large, multi-division corporations in this context. There is certainly much to be said for presidential participation with major customers if the corporation is small enough for the top person to know the chief businesses in considerable detail. At General Instrument, Chairman and President Hickey takes an active part in selling efforts, particularly on behalf of GI's cable television equipment operations. The principal customers are few in number, so individual attention by the head of the corporation is possible, and cable television products represent half of General Instrument's sales volume, so their success is of great importance. Finally, and not usual for a chief executive, Hickey not only enjoys such direct exchanges with customers, but he is also very effective at it.

With respect to product and customer orientation, at bottom these are business planning matters, not to be unilaterally decided between the headquarters vice president marketing and the new acquisition.

At the same time, headquarters marketing will want to have a say in advertising and sales promotion activities, perhaps joint participation with sister divisions in trade shows. There may be a corporate identification program with a new logo, common appearance of signs on buildings, even a common stationery color.

All these things are too frequently pressed upon a new acquisition as if they were of monumental importance. They are not, despite some headquarters marketing or public relations people who will strenuously argue the opposite.

Therefore, bringing most of the new entity's marketing practices into line with corporate standards can be accomplished with all deliberate speed. Don't do it pell mell, causing unnecessary friction and mistrust between headquarters and the new division, to the detriment of future mutual support.

5
TECHNOLOGY AND MANUFACTURING

THE LEVEL OF COMPETENCE in an operating unit's engineering activities is the most difficult of all for a corporate HQ staff to evaluate. The reason is clear. It takes from five to ten years for an engineer to become really good at his design or application specialty. And when he has reached that peak, who is to judge whether or not his ideas, or their execution, is good, bad, or indifferent? Who is competent to conduct a design review of his newest product specifications and drawings, or critique his application yeas or nays?

A power transformer engineer, for example, spends years learning and practicing his craft and finally masters it as well as anyone can. Now his design ideas are respected in his company and industry as representing the best state of the art available. But can he tomorrow become an ace fractional-horsepower motor designer or a microelectronics chip application engineer? Obviously not.

To become an expert engineer in any of those other fields, he would have to learn the specialty from the ground up, and another five or ten years pass. This is why engineers are so difficult to transfer from one corporate division to another. Easy for financial people—general accounting and cost accounting principles are much the same in any business. Less easy, but still feasible for marketing and manufacturing people. It's the poor engineer whose skills are not transferable without a long apprentice period in the new field.

Therefore, the only person capable of rendering really good judgment on an engineer's work is another engineer who is expert in the same field. Does there exist anywhere a corporate HQ staff possessing really expert engineers in *all* the corporation's businesses? No, not even in the largest headquarters.

Yet there is nothing more important for the continuing life of a multi-division manufacturing corporation than high-quality technological ability: in generating new product ideas; in getting them from the drawing board into production; in communicating application know-how to the sales force and customers; in overcoming production and quality problems; in making intelligent cost reductions; and in correctly evaluating technological evolution in its product fields. Mistakes in engineering judgment have cost many corporations dearly over the years, and even put some out of business altogether.

But aren't the division engineers, including their managers, on top of what's going on in their field? If they are doing their job, shouldn't the division general managers and corporate HQ be protected against technological mistakes? In theory, yes. In practice, a lot of engineering goes wrong. Why?

Engineers are generally an intellectually arrogant lot. Engineering schools are tough. The mental discipline and effort required to get a degree is greater, let's admit it, than that required for a degree in accounting, or journalism, or political science. So engineers have the feeling that their mental powers are superior to those of people in most other professions. This being their belief, they are reluctant to consider any other product ideas as possibly better than their own. This is the deadly NIH (not-invented-here) factor.

Examples: while sales manager of instrument transformers with General Electric, I had the good fortune to be in on the introduction of molded transformers. These were a great step forward over earlier designs, and our share of available market went from 30 to 50 percent in just three years.

One of the best features of the new transformer was the replacement of porcelain bushings (which can chip and break) with a molded plastic material considerably more rugged. Since GE's lightning arrester business used porcelain housings, many of which could be advantageously replaced by molded plastics, we suggested the the lightning arrester people take a good look at what had been accomplished in instrument transformers.

The response was a long list of detailed reasons why the molded bushing approach held no interest for lightning arresters. The plastics couldn't replace porcelain for many reasons. The upshot—not until ten years later did General Electric's lightning arrester people embrace molded housings and bushings, finally aroused to action by the most potent of energizing forces, competition getting an edge in the marketplace by going to molded plastics first. That's the harmful effect of engineering NIH dogmatism.

Even worse is when engineering has the sales force battle competitors on technological grounds that turn out to be plain wrong. Such a case was GE's transformer division fighting the introduction by Westinghouse of dry-type transformers. The new Westinghouse designs offered worthwhile advantages. They were lighter and had no danger of leaks, and thus involved no fire hazard, whereas the liquid used in most older designs was oil. But the General Electric transformer engineers were totally committed to liquid-filled transformers. They fought dry-type transformers for years, producing learned documents for marketing to use with customers. The papers "proved" that dry-type transformers would never make the grade, because they were inherently unreliable and would have at best a very short life.

The conclusion: Westinghouse demonstrated that actual customer experience wins out over adverse propaganda. By the time GE faced up to the fact that dry-type transformers were here to stay and began to produce them, Westinghouse had seized the lead in its share of the transformer market.

So we are faced with a very real problem. Correct evaluation of technology, where it is and where it is going, can make or break a corporation's individual businesses. Yet technology is an area where only the best practitioners are capable of adequately judging the quality of work by other engineers in the same field. So how does a multi-division corporation's staff fulfill its necessary functions of evaluating line engineering performance for top management?

This is one of the few situations where one can readily sympathize with corporate staff, because the fact is they *cannot* do this important task adequately. The best they can do is an after-the-fact monitoring of what actually happens to new products, new application ideas, *after* they have been launched in the marketplace. The correctness of engineers' evaluation of technological trends, and the direction their perceptions then give to new product programs, is usually clear only in hindsight.

Staunch believers in scientific management will no doubt dispute this view. They will point out that the entire planning and budgeting process each year, as well as regular operations reviews as a year progresses, give HQ staff and top management ample opportunity to weigh new and ongoing engineering projects. Management can see what is actually happening and avoid costly errors in engineering judgment by selecting the most promising projects for implementation, putting added emphasis on those that are going well, and aborting those that falter during implementation.

It will be readily seen that the last two "controls," adding effort to ventures that are going well and stopping those going badly, are de facto hindsight actions. The only one calling for foresight by staff is evaluation of *new* engineering proposals. A critical area, yes, and how good can HQ staff and top management be at it?

Let's begin at the top. In today's multi-division, large corporation, no president or chief operating officer can really claim to understand the technological evolution going on in all the corporation's businesses. Nor can the planning vice president. Even one of the most hardworking large corporation heads of recent years, Harold Geneen, couldn't do it, though he tried mightily.

When Geneen became ITT's president in 1960, the corporation's chief business was telecommunications equipment, followed by electronic components used in such equipment. Within several years, Geneen could talk design and application detail for such products as an equal with all but a few of ITT's top engineers. A remarkable achievement, seldom repeated or even attempted by large corporation presidents.

But, as ITT acquired and acquired new businesses throughout the 1960s, even a Harold Geneen was overwhelmed. ITT got into heating and air conditioning, motors and pumps, radar equipment, printing, home construction, paper production, wire and cable, radio and TV sets, automobile parts—you name it: ITT had it. Geneen could still talk a good fight on almost any product's technology, but it didn't carry the conviction of knowledge in depth that his earlier mastery of telecommunications equipment had.

So the task is hopeless for a multi-division corporation's chief executive and planning officer, even aided and coached by staff, to be really meaningfully on top of all the technological choices being made in the corporation, before trial by actual results takes place.

The only exceptions are those where the entrepreneur who started the business, frequently an engineer, and who knows every aspect of the trade, is still the president. Yet even such detailed expertise, high intelligence, and outstanding energy levels as such people possess are not fault-proof. Even a Robert Noyce, founder of Intel, or a Charles Sporck, president of National Semiconductor, admit to having made product acceptance or market growth miscalculations from time to time, though their overall batting average is remarkably high.

Have we therefore reached a dead end? If top management and engineering people on HQ staff can't adequately evaluate or guide divisional engineering choices and decisions regarding technological evolution in the corporation's businesses, what then? Outside consultants who are technology experts in a particular division's field can help some. But their contribution is double-edged. They, too, are intellectually arrogant, suffer from the NIH syndrome, frequently have favorite technological axes to grind, and sometimes have trouble remembering which matters are confidential.

What is left at bottom is the line technical people in the divisions, and they must do the job largely on their own. This means that the corporation's best protection, best insurance against failure, and best chance of success is to try to ensure that the line engineers in each division are the finest available, or at least within shouting distance.

The situation is excellent if the division general manager is the entrepreneur who started the business; good if the GM has grown up in the business and knows its evolution and pace from direct experience; better if, in addition, the GM has an engineering background.

At General Electric's management school in Croton-on-Hudson, a philosophy of management was taught that could be summarized as, "A good general manager can manage any kind of business." But that is simplistic. Every business has its own ambience: a unique history, a specific technological evolution, a certain lineup of competitors, a particular group of customers with changing needs, its own pace and style of doing business. All these things can be learned and absorbed in time. But it does take time, even for a talented individual. The General Electric management philosophy should say, "A good general manager can manage any kind of business, in time, eventually." But what happens in the meantime?

The dangers are especially great where the technology in a particular field is supremely important. GE tried to give its management school philosophy a practical demonstration when its computer division was established in Phoenix. The first general manager was from the automotive industry. He was followed shortly by the manager of

General Electric's own outdoor lighting division. Then, equally shortly, by their general manager from the light military equipment division.

Finally the light dawned, and a new general manager was brought in from the computer industry, but it was too late to join the leaders, who were by then far ahead. Twenty years later, after having poured many millions of dollars into a lost cause, GE withdrew from the computer battle, except for industrial process control applications.

So the key to the problem is having good technical knowledge at the divisions. If there exists real competent engineering talent on the headquarters staff, put it out in the divisions where it can do some direct good for the corporation. A research laboratory maintained and directed by HQ? Perhaps. A few technical experts on HQ staff keeping an eye on technologies not now in use in the corporation that may be of significance in the future? All right, but the best answers to the technological dilemma at multi-division corporate HQ is to try to ensure that the divisions are staffed with engineers good in their field, and then let them get on with the job with a minimum of interference.

Now what about the handling by HQ of a new acquisition's technical situation? From all the above, the basics should be clear. Attempts to monitor and control the acquisition's technical people directly should not be made. They will prove ineffectual and are potentially damaging: through unnecessary delays in projects where time may be of the essence; through alienation of key technical people, an unruly breed at best; through diversion of a valuable resource—engineering time—to projects suggested offhand by a staff person over a cup of coffee.

For a new acquisition the use by HQ of outside consultants to evaluate its engineering/technical competence is also bad, at least for the first year or two. Such an action will be interpreted as lack of confidence, adding yet another unnecessary strain to the already difficult task of establishing productive working relationships between HQ and the new division.

The time for evaluation of the technological competence of a new entity is *before* the company is acquired. Without divulging acquisitive intentions, the corporation can learn all it needs to know about the state of the technology of a potential new member of its family. First and most important, as perceived by customers of the possible acquisition. Then from its competitors, field representatives and distributors, and technical consultants to the acquisition's industry.

Then, following acquisition, the corporate staff extends its understanding of the new division's technology through the business planning and budgeting process, followed by operations reviews of what is actually happening as the fiscal year proceeds. Thus, with patience and good will, the corporate HQ will reach an adequate level of understanding of the new baby's technological competence by year two or three, meanwhile having avoided the problems created by a too eager jump into the technological area peculiar to the new division.

The most effective engineering in the world, of course, falls flat if translating the design ideas into a finished product is faulty. This is where manufacturing competence moves to the forefront.

In many ways, manufacturing is the most difficult of all business functions. Besides working with reams of paper and numbers and having to marshall and coordinate the efforts of many people, manufacturing involves physical handling of all too real materials and processes. Materials and processes that exasperatingly frequently exhibit recalcitrance to behaving in intended ways. The pieces don't go together neatly as they should according to the engineering drawings. Complex processes don't produce the desired end result.

Other functions are not sympathetic enough to all these difficulties. Sales demands shorter shipment times and 100 percent realization of promised shipment dates. Engineering produces designs that are beyond the capability of manufacturing's present equipment to meet. Their aim is to "push" manufacturing's state of the art, requiring financial outlays for new capital equipment so their specifications can be met. Finance takes a dim view of the money tied up in inventories and objects to the amount of overtime money being spent in the factory to meet those promised shipment dates.

The conscientious manufacturing person can never get ahead of the game. The best one can hope for is to stay largely abreast of the inevitable crises that erupt regularly from some direction or other. The end-of-line automatic testing machine breaks down, so completed product is piling up behind it. A key supplier falls behind on delivery of a critical piece-part, threatening to close down the factory completely. A walkout of tool makers is imminent because of some unsettled grievance. The welding machines on line b are proving incapable of maintaining the higher production rate called for by production control. And engineering is insisting that quality control limits on acceptable finished product be tightened to half their existing level. Manufacturing people are *busy*.

Now the manufacturing people in Alpha Company learn that they are being acquired by Omega Corporation. Their reaction is, So what? Top executives may be changed, finance has to get used to a whole new ball game of more frequent and more detailed reporting, but won't it be business as usual in production control and on the shop floor? No it won't.

The initial shock comes when manufacturing learns that a substantial part of the new reporting to Omega's corporate HQ is detailed manufacturing information. It seems that the headquarters at Omega must be full of manufacturing experts. They want to know each month the productivity and the efficiency of direct labor engaged on each of the new acquisition's product lines; the percentage of shipment promises met; the ratio of direct to indirect labor in the plant; savings realized on cost reduction projects; new tooling and equipment expenditures made or committed to be made; the numbers of new hires during the month, along with the numbers who left or were dismissed, with a reason for each one.

Of course much of this flow of information is already being generated. The acquisition's management, especially in manufacturing, needs it in order to plan and manage effectively. But you can be sure the information is not at present being produced in the format requested. Rearrangement of information is required, perhaps involving change in the way, or the time cycle, in which the information is gathered.

Example: the great productivity vs. efficiency debate, and how to calculate them. What is productivity? The acquisition has been calculating productivity as standard hours paid divided by total hours paid to employees *working directly* on production lines. This excludes the hours when production workers are not actually on the line but are busy elsewhere, perhaps doing clean-up work, or lending a hand in the shipping department because of deadlines to be met. But Omega Corporation mandates that those nonproduction line hours be included in the calculation. This, of course, produces a lower productivity number.

If that is productivity, what is efficiency? The new parent says that efficiency is standard hours earned divided by standard hours paid. But the acquired entity has not been making this kind of calculation at all. It has been dividing the numerator of the parent's efficiency computation by the denominator of its productivity calculation, and calling the result efficiency.

Confusing? If you understood the two preceding paragraphs on first reading, then you immediately qualify as an expert on the fine distinctions that can be made in evaluating manufacturing activities. The aquisition is confused, too, so has trouble getting into gear to report as their new boss headquarters mandates.

Meanwhile, a staff manufacturing expert shows up from corporate HQ to get acquainted and do his evaluation duty as to the effectiveness of the new entity's manufacturing operations. Not surprisingly, much of what is going on he views with alarm.

The new division has built its business by doing considerable customizing of product, especially for large customers. This willingness and ability to customize has earned it the unique niche it enjoys in its industry and is an important reason why it was considered a good acquisition to make in the first place. But the staff manufacturing man came from a business that concentrates on turning out millions of widgets all exactly alike—"Any color you want as long as it's black," This approach makes possible low production costs and has worked well for his alma mater.

So he points out the obvious to the manufacturing people at the acquisition. "Your production runs are too short. Too many variations in the product types. You have to change tooling too often, and you could use much higher-speed production equipment simply by cutting out a lot of your product variations."

The staff expert then turns his attention to inventory, a perennially thorny problem in any business organization. "Good God," he says, "inventory turns only three times a year! That's ridiculously low. It should be at least five or six times a year. Just ask your accountant how much it costs to carry that much inventory!" The thought of such waste of corporate money lends righteous indignation to his expostulations.

"But," object the acquisition's people, "the reason inventory turns are so low is the variety of product types we have to be prepared to manufacture on short notice." "Precisely," says the HQ man, "get rid of all that product variety, and you will get both lower manufacturing costs and reduced inventory."

Now what are the manufacturing people of the acquisition supposed to do with such sweeping recommendations? Clearly the new entity's management is not going to agree readily that the entire product strategy—customizing—that has made them successful is to be junked because of a staff expert's quick analysis and recommendations.

But those recommendations can't be ignored—because on returning to HQ the manufacturing expert writes a report on what he saw, how sad it was, and what he recommended to the new division's manufacturing people be done about the "problem." Overnight the acquisition's successful strategy in its marketplace becomes a problem as seen by headquarters manufacturing staff.

Now begins the wasteful push and haul so common in large corporations, taking time and energy away from getting on with the basic job of producing good financial results while satisfying customers.

Getting a copy of the manufacturing man's exposé, the group vice president at HQ to whom the acquisition reports asks for comments from the new division general manager. The GM, wanting to make a balanced and up-to-date response, involves all his functions in developing a reply. This precipitates a new, or revives an old controversy within the previously independent company.

The manufacturing manager states that of course the HQ staff man is right. "I've never liked all this variety of product types we have to contend with. It's inefficient in the factory, and it drives our production control people up the wall!" The engineering manager is torn. He is proud of his group's engineering ability to modify the basic product to meet customer desires, which may actually be needs. He has sat in meetings with his chief customers and enjoyed the technical challenge of finding ways to do what they want. On the other hand he recognizes the engineering workload reduction that product simplification would bring, allowing more time to be spent on new product development projects dear to his heart.

The financial manager doesn't have a definite opinion. She asks the key questions: "Will we be able to get the same sales volume without customizing? Or will we get enough cost reductions in manufacturing to offset possible sales loss?" This passes the ball to the marketing manager, who is apoplectic. "What the hell is all this nonsense?" she shouts. "We are a successful company largely *because* of customization. And here we sit casually discussing throwing our marketing strategy out the window, just because some fool from HQ, a manufacturing man, says to do so . . . (sputter...sputter) . . . ridiculous!"

Well, the beleaguered general manager finally sides with the marketing manager and drafts a reply to his new boss at HQ. Since they don't yet know each other very well, the reply is couched in careful terms: "Interesting ideas . . . will give them careful consideration . . . examining potential benefits and problems of such basic changes . . . " etc., etc.

Meanwhile the marketing manager seeks understanding from someone on the marketing staff at HQ, preferably the vice president of marketing. If she's lucky, she'll find a good advocate at headquarters who has been a successful practitioner of customizing. If she's not lucky, it will be a long, cold winter.

Imbroglios such as the above take their toll in diverting valuable management time and effort from the business at hand. But the damage that can be wrought by one manufacturing staff expert in just one "get acquainted" visit is small when compared with the reverberations from the initial visit by a HQ planning person. The effect is nicely magnified, of course, if the distinguished visitor happens to be the corporation's vice president for planning.

But why should the new division's manufacturing activities come quickly to the fore in an initial review by the HQ planning people? It comes about this way. At some point during the course of discussion, the HQ planning person asks, "How long have you been producing product at this location?" "Twenty-five years," proudly answers the general manager. "Adequate supply of labor?" "Oh yes, no problem." "Union relations?" "Stable," says the GM. "What is your base labor cost per hour?" "About $6.00 base, $7.50 with fringes."

"There you are," says the HQ planning expert, leaning forward, "labor costs are much too high. Have you considered moving your plant to Taiwan?" "What . . . what?" gulps the division manager. "Yes, indeed," continues the planner, "labor costs on Taiwan are only $2.00 per hour base, $3.25 with fringes. You told me earlier that you utilize some 1 million direct labor hours annually. At a $4.25 differential per hour, you could save $4.25 million per year. You could, therefore," he concludes triumphantly, "increase your pretax income by 50 percent."

The general manager sits there stunned by this quick-brush treatment of a very complex matter, as he hears the planner conclude, "Well, I'll be on my way. Give the idea serious consideration, because I'm going to recommend it at HQ."

Obviously, any consideration of closing a plant is a very serious matter indeed. Nothing causes more tremors in an organization than alarm about the possibility that what is here today may be gone in six months. This justified alarm affects not just the people on the factory floor, but all functions and all levels.

If manufacturing operations move to Taiwan, of course the people on the production lines lose their jobs, but what about the support functions? Is production control, industrial engineering, maintenance and repairs, the tool room, quality control, all going to Taiwan? Seems logical they should. What about design engineering? How good will future designs and application engineering be if the engineers are physically located 8,000 miles from the factory? Even finance is affected. General accounting may remain in the United States, but surely cost accounting belongs at the factory.

While deliberations are going on at the top management level in the division, weighing the pros and cons of the HQ planning person's Taiwan initiative, can the morale problems that follow widespread knowledge that such a move is even under consideration be avoided? No, they cannot. One or more of the top managers will alert various people. "Guess what those nuts at corporate HQ have proposed for us?" Its just too juicy a secret to be kept.

But even if the local managers keep the matter close to their chests, the HQ people will announce it to their opposite numbers at the division. "Say, I understand you guys are moving to Taiwan," says a headquarters financial analyst to the startled division's chief cost accountant, anxious to let the new people know that he is privy to top-level corporate matters. So the story spreads throughout the new division. Its good people start considering their options. Résumés are circulated. The less secure members of the organization sink into despondency.

Meanwhile the acquired company's general manager, made of stern stuff, is massing reasons why such a move would not really be helpful. He finds plenty of them. His own best people in engineering and manufacturing are not about to agree to move themselves or their families to Taiwan. Thus, if such a move were made, a new engineering organization would have to be created. The experienced corps of engineers who have made the division a leader in its field would dissipate, many going to competitors.

To be replaced by what? Either by American or European engineers who, transferred to Taiwan, would have to be paid considerably more that their counterparts in the United States, or by Taiwanese engineers, smart and hardworking, but who would have a long way to go to match their predecessors' expertise.

This basic problem, more salary money or less experience, carried through all functions, would go far to negate the direct labor saving. Especially since, in most manufacturing organizations, the dollars spent on direct labor are considerably less than those spent on salaried people.

Add to this picture the new higher costs of freight, both vendor supplied material going out to Taiwan and finished product returning; larger inventories needed because of the longer supply pipeline; heavy travel and living expenses for people from the States going back and forth to resolve myriad production and engineering problems magnified by the distance; ditto Taiwanese coming to the old plant location to observe and learn before being put on their own.

The most persistant cost problem, however, is duplication of activities. When operations are moved to Taiwan, or any other remote location, *no* American corporation really bites the bullet and makes its manufacturing operations totally local in the new place. Examples are quality control, shipping and receiving, purchasing, order entry, and production control.

The U.S. corporation has to have quality control at the Far Eastern factory, of course, but it also keeps—for years—duplicate QC people at the old home location. To be certain, you see, that the quality level passed by the new plant's quality people is really OK. Shipping and receiving is necessary at the new factory, but it also has to be retained at the old location. Suppliers send their piece-parts to the U.S. location, where they are unpacked and tested by QC people, then repacked and sent to the Asian factory. Finished goods from the new factory come first to the old location, where they are unpacked and again tested by the home QC people, then finally repacked and sent on to customers. You get the idea. This duplication goes on for five to ten years, while management wonders, "Where are the savings we expected?"

If such a quickly recommended move is actually implemented by the acquisition, the headquarters planning man's assumption of over 4 million dollars cost savings goes up in smoke. Postmortems will search for the reasons. Heads may roll at the division because of "faulty implementation." Meanwhile the planning man will be doing business as usual, now suggesting to another hapless division manager that operations be moved to Singapore.

An aside is appropriate here. I do not maintain that all such moves of manufacturing operations to the Far East or Mexico are mistakes. But the accumulated experience of American industry over the past 20 years shows that such moves are all too often undertaken with woefully inadequate consideration of the total cost effect. The focus has been on immediate direct labor savings, easy to calculate.

Even for labor costs, insufficient attention has been given to how fast those direct labor rates were likely to rise relative to the United States. Over the past ten years U.S. labor rates in manufacturing have risen an average 7 percent per year, while Taiwanese direct labor costs have been rising 20 to 25 percent each year. Taiwanese labor costs are still lower today that those in the United States, but taking all the other *increased* cost factors into consideration, cost reduction per se is not a convincing reason to move plants to the Far East.

But our subject is proper care and integrating of a new acquisition. How do we protect the fledgling division's manufacturing operations from such disruptive or untimely interference by the parent HQ staff people?

The first and most important rule is to use the business planning process to review and evaluate the acquisition's manufacturing operations. Seldom does it have to be done in a hurry, early in the new division's tenure. Over the normal six months or so of a business planning cycle, the details of the acquisition's manufacturing operations—expected cost reductions, desired tooling and equipment expenditure, production control techniques—will be spelled out in considerable detail in the new division's initial business plan.

Perusing and then discussing the plan with the division's manufacturing people give HQ staff plenty of opportunity to comment on and question why various things are handled as they are. This is the time for the staff manufacturing expert to inquire into length of product runs, inventory turns, productivity and efficiency, and to make recommendations about them.

Over the same period of time the headquarters marketing people will be considering the division's strategy of customization for large customers, and its record of success. Thus, when final review of the plan takes place at HQ, the marketing people will be able to have their say about the advisability of following the manufacturing expert's desire to throw out customization. The division will not in the meantime have been stirred up to unnecessary and unproductive turmoil because of unilateral, one-function, suggestions from staff people.

The second rule is that any really earth-shaking suggestions from HQ, such as, "Why not move to Taiwan," should never be made off-the-cuff. If any manufacturing changes, for example, involving closing a plant and starting a new one, seem appropriate, they should be broached to the new acquisition only after the careful consideration made by the parent corporation's top executives while wearing sackcloth and ashes. And then they should be discussed at first only with the cognizant general manager of the new division.

The basic manufacturing job is to produce products in its plant or plants and ship them out the door to customers. There is a constant stream of activity revolving around continuing to make items that have been produced before, and adding newly designed or modified items as engineering releases them to the factory.

Thus the foremost concern of manufacturing is the ability of the tools, equipment and processes it has to work with to produce the product in accordance with engineering's specifications. If the finished product meets its engineering specifications, as measured by quality control checks and tests, then by definition it is a quality product.

An active manufacturing organization displays an insatiable appetite for new tooling and equipment, always with the same aim, to be able to produce the product faster, easier, and more surely meeting the engineering specifications. Thus it is that the list of capital spending wants generated by manufacturing organizations is always impressively long, and almost always exceeds the amount of capital spending money available from a prudent cash flow budget.

This is particularly so when new products are to be introduced into the stream. Engineering, trying to demonstrate technical excellence, impress customers, and give one in the eye to competitors—all things that sales applauds vigorously—produces specifications for the new products that can't be met by existing equipment in the plant. Manufacturing, for its part, has found through experience with existing products which parts of the current manufacturing process are most likely to cause trouble. For these areas they want new and better tools to work with.

Dealing with the wish list at business planning and budgeting time is a perennial headache for division management. The urgent claims of manufacturing have to be balanced against monetary requirements of all other functions. And, of course, that wish list doesn't remain fixed. Priorities change: because engineering release of a new product is delayed; because production rates have to be quickly raised on a best seller; because a serious breakdown moves preventive maintenance of old equipment ahead of implementation of some otherwise worthwhile bright ideas.

Now the previously independent company, newly acquired, has been dealing with these things all along, so where is the problem? The problem is the introduction of new players into the loop. The HQ people who will now be part of the game.

That wish list from manufacturing introduced into the business planning and budgeting process of the parent corporation causes much more trouble than it should, especially if the corporation keeps a tight rein on the amount of capital spending money that can be committed by a division on its own. An extreme, no doubt, is the example of General Instrument. All through the 1970s, GI top management required all division capital spending requests over $5,000 to be reviewed by staff, and then to receive final approval by the president himself. This in a corporation whose larger divisions were normally spending millions of dollars a year on capital equipment and tooling projects.

Does such a minuscule local approval level make sense? In 1980 the Clare division of General Instrument sent 102 capital spending appropriation requests to GI headquarters in New York. Ten of these represented 75 percent of the total monies requested and so of course were the important projects deserving staff and presidential attention. But the other 92 (25 percent of the funds requested) required nine times as much staff time as the major projects, because of the detailed review required and the $5,000 limit for local approval of any capital expense.

Even with a more reasonable limit for local approval, the introduction of headquarters staff review into the picture causes delay and frustration for a new acquisition. The headquarters people will be trying to learn all they can about the new business, and close scrutiny and cross-examination of capital spending programs is a good avenue to understanding. But the acquired people have jobs to do and want to get on with them. It will seem inconceivable to them that if an important piece of production equipment needs replacing they must petition headquarters for approval.

On the other side, of course, staff people can show you examples of the most remarkable nonsense received from divisions, ostensibly supporting proposed capital expenditures. This lack of coherence sometimes in divisional requests for capital money outlays, of even very large amounts, leads to overkill on the part of staff when making their review. Suddenly the HQ big picture of the forest becomes a close look at trees and even bushes in questioning the need, timing, and amount of the proposed expenditures.

Various corporate controls and limits on capital spending by manufacturing and engineering in the divisions are appropriate, of course. Basically however, after-the-fact reviews of division decisions in this area are sufficient protection for headquarters, except for the largest programs, which should require advance approval.

The above applies particularly in the case of an acquisition, which will be buffeted sufficiently by all the added requirements and constraints involved in its relationship with the new parent corporation. A minimum of interference with the normal flow of engineering and manufacturing in the new division is especially needed in the beginning, while the headquarters staff people become better informed, step by step, as to what the entity is doing and why. This measured approach saves time and unnecessary trouble for both the new division and headquarters.

6

INTERNATIONAL
OPERATIONS

ALMOST ALL CORPORATIONS today are involved in operations outside the headquarters' home country. Those who don't have directly owned and operated subsidiaries in foreign countries will have multi-national connections in some form. There will be licensing arrangements with manufacturers of similar products; agents or distributors who will be selling products imported from the home country; buy/sell agreements where the home corporation imports from other countries and resells; perhaps joint ventures in research and development.

Therefore, today there is a considerable degree of experience and expertise among most manufacturing companies in regard to the complications and frustrations of doing business across national boundaries: language barriers; the parochialism of any entity heightened dramatically by nationalistic feelings (as often pretended as real, but a potent factor); differing trade practices; national or local trade associations with specifications and acceptance testing controls; customs regulations; new sets of taxing and regulating authorities.

We need to consider two different situations in the context of acquisitions: where the acquirer buys a U.S. company that has operating subsidiaries in other countries, and where the acquirer buys an independent company in a foreign country.

Where the foreign entities are already subsidiaries of a U.S. company, the situation is helped by things already in existence. The foreign operations will be familiar with the U.S. parent wanting all financial reports to headquarters to be expressed in U.S. dollars, not local currency. They will already know U.S. style business planning. Accommodations with the U.S. parent's personnel and benefit policies will have already been made.

When a U.S. corporation acquires a previously independent foreign company, however, the situation is much more difficult. The acquiring corporation will have to undertake the task of overcoming all the problems inherent in the integration of any acquisition, with the job made ten times more difficult because of the across-borders complications, and the sometimes unpleasant aspects of nationalistic feeling.

What is different in approaching the integration of entities in other countries as compared with our earlier discussions? What are the extra dimensions introduced by the "foreign" element in the picture?

Let's assume the acquisition is a European company and begin with language differences, which can cause a lot of trouble. That is the chief reason why telex rather than telephone is used so much more in Europe than in the States, when communicating across national boundaries. You have a written record, so the language can be mulled over and translated carefully before you reply.

We Americans are very fortunate that English is almost a universal language in international business: everywhere in the English-speaking world of course, including all the former British colonies like India, Pakistan, Nigeria; everywhere in Western Europe; the second language all over Asia; and neck and neck with German as the second language in Eastern Europe.

So where is the language problem? It is that though you can be almost certain that top people in the acquired company will speak passable English, this is not so for middle and lower management and even less so on the shop floor. Yet it is going to be necessary for many people in headquarters and other corporate operations to be able to communicate directly with their opposite numbers at the new subsidiary: marketing people, engineers, manufacturing people all will need to communicate more or less frequently. So the answer, like it or not, is that many of the subsidiary's people must learn English.

Even without urging or prodding, the best, most ambitious people in the new entity will learn English on their own, and fast. They'll say to themselves, "If I'm going to progress in this outfit, English it has to be, so let's get on with it." But for others, management must insist on the English: provide lessons and total immersion seminars; practice meetings all in English; require reports written in English.

If this seems harsh or unreasonable, consider the alternative. If we go the other way and say the American headquarters people should learn the foreign language, the sobering question is, Which language? The acquiring corporation will probably have operations in Germany, France, Italy, the Scandinavian countries, South America, Asia. Which language? The only possible answer is English. Also consider an international meeting of, say, the corporation's European engineers. There will be representatives from Sweden, Spain, Germany, Switzerland, Italy, and France. What language will they have to use in the meeting? English, of course. Lucky for us; for others, that's the way it is.

As we've reviewed earlier, any acquired company's employees will be nervous and suspicious of what will happen under the new regime. This difficulty standing in the way of harmonious integration of a new entity into a larger corporate structure is made much greater when the acquisition is a formerly independent company in a foreign country. Now the normal tendencies to friction and frustration are greatly exacerbated by all the nationalistic phobias that can possibly be conjured up, and they are legion. The rumors will flow steadily: "We were bought only in order to close us down." "No more engineering will be done here—all in the States." "Only engineering will be done here. All manufacturing will be moved to Taiwan or Korea." "Our books are going to be falsified, to avoid paying local taxes." "Our pension fund has already been transferred to New York and will be spent by the people there." "No Frenchman (or German, or Englishman) is allowed to get ahead in this corporation. They hate French people."

The problem of suspicion of motives extends to all areas. Initiate discussion of what form of legal entity for the new acquisition is most appropriate to the overall corporate legal structure, and the acquisition's lawyers will be sure you have some dishonorable intention, usually assumed to be tax avoidance.

Ask about the new entity's sources of supply for its key components, and be treated to a lecture on why changing any of them will be impossible. Inquire into the rationale behind the company's organizational structure, and be told that Americans simply do not understand the way Europeans think.

Besides these general difficulties, there are a particular set of problems associated with establishing good relationships with each functional area of the business. Let's look at them, beginning with finance.

Fortunately, the numbers will look the same to everyone. The Arabic numeric system is used everywhere, even in Arabia, and by and large companies everywhere keep the same kinds of books. There will be differences in charts of accounts, of course, differences in depreciation calculations, differences in the way cost sheets are made up. But at bottom, between the mutually understood numbers, and sign language if necessary, the financial people from headquarters and those of the new subsidiary will be able to communicate.

The first extra burden for the acquisition's financial people is the necessity for duplicate financial reports at all levels of the foreign subsidiary. It is not only at the consolidated level, P & L and balance sheet, that translation into U.S. dollars must be made. At headquarters, manufacturing experts want material and labor cost sheets and quality control costs expressed in dollars. The physical inventory records of buildings, tools, and equipment, down to the last desk and typewriter, have to be expressed in both local currency and U.S. dollars.

Never mind how often the foreign subsidiary inquires why the top managers at headquarters can't learn to think in terms of local currencies. No matter that the subsidiary correctly points out that performance measurements should be based on results expressed in local currency, eliminating currency fluctuation distortions. The fact is that U.S. managers will look at financial reports translated into dollars, period; and Siemens top brass in Germany looks at Deutsche marks; and Matsushita in Tokyo looks at yen. It's a fact of life.

The next extra burden for financial people is the necessity of explaining the effect of currency exchange fluctuations, which cause a lot of confusion. The runs up and down in European currency values relative to the dollar and relative to each other of the past ten years are unprecedented in the history of modern industrialized nations.

When the exchange rate of the Belgian franc goes from 40 to the dollar to only 30 in two years, a 25 percent change in favor of the franc, a Belgian subsidiary looks great to its U.S. parent. Whatever changes are occurring in the actual business, expressed in local currency, are improved 25 percent when translated into U.S. dollars. Sales, rising at say 10 percent per year in real terms, seem to have leaped up over 50 percent in two years when translated into U.S. dollars. Marvelous! The U.S. parent is impressed.

But it is to be hoped the managers in Belgium are modest. Because, in the ensuing two years the Belgian franc goes *back* from 30 to 40 to the dollar. Ouch! The sales may be still rising 10 percent per year in real terms in local currency, but translated into U.S. dollars they now look as though they are *dropping.* What on earth has happened to that nice operation in Belgium? Heads are shaking sadly all over headquarters in New York. The managers in Belgium now try to engage in a crash course of instruction on the pernicious effects of currency fluctuations for the benefit of the U.S. parent, but they find the going tough.

A very real difficulty for previously independent European companies becoming subsidiaries of a large U.S. corporation is accepting the need for spreading financial information throughout the company. Until now the financial figures have been very closely held within the accounting function, shared only with a few top officials.

This preoccupation with financial secrecy seems strange to American managers, who don't believe intelligent forecasting and business planning can be done unless the tasks are shared by many people in the organization: sales, engineering, manufacturing, as well as finance, all in possession of the facts about financial results, past, present, and expected future. Nor does an American manager see how useful reviews of current operations can take place in a vacuum, that is, if knowledge of the financial results of those operations is not shared by all the participants.

The previously independent European top manager, though, and the financial officer, will find adjusting to the open American style a difficult transition. This is best accomplished step by step, beginning with business planning and budgeting, and then progressing to review of actual results vs. plan and budget. The European managers will then see how planning and operating in accordance with the U.S. parent's style *requires* widespread participation on the process by many people in the organization, and how that participation, to be effective, must utilize considerable financial information.

Because of all these factors, the previous advice concerning how to integrate an acquisition's financial activity into that of the new parent acquires greater significance, since the foreign financial function is already operating under considerable handicaps.

Accordingly, the changes now required—to a new corporate chart of accounts and new reporting schedules, probably with additional detail in the reports, all requiring changes in the existing modus operandi not of just the financial function but of all functions—should be handled slowly and carefully. Not dropping bombs of new accounting manuals, new forms and instructions, and new reporting schedules on the hapless foreign subsidiary for as-soon-as-possible implementation. Rather the three-step approach: first, explaining what changes will be necessary and why; second, laying out a reasonable timetable for carrying out the changes in good order; and finally, reviewing progress together with the new subsidiary's financial people, and adjusting implementation schedules as appropriate. For a realistic timetable, double that required for a U.S. operation.

Since the acquisition was previously a wholly European company, the marketing people at the parent HQ will probably find that its sales effort is heavily concentrated in the home country: France, Germany, or Great Britain. Even today, it is usually only the largest European corporations, themselves multi-division, multi-national companies, who operate across national borders with the same ease as even smaller American companies.

The Common Market (European Economic Community) has done a lot to encourage across-borders business dealings, and to minimize customs duties and other barriers to trade within Europe. Still, national specification organizations, or testing laboratories, whose approval is required before a foreign company can sell locally, can and do slow the efforts of foreign competitors. Language is also an ever present impediment.

Beyond such visible barriers, there lies a more important difficulty, and that is national prejudices. Northern Europeans look down on southern European countries. The French and Belgians have deep-rooted worries about the Germans. The English feel somehow superior to everyone else. These feelings, irrational as they may appear today, do exist.

All these considerations explain why the European acquisition concentrates on the home country, and why its sales efforts across borders may seem tentative and slow to an American.

The acquiring corporation will naturally want its new subsidiary to reach out and duplicate its home sales effort in other countries. Changing the existing situation quickly is seldom possible, however. The HQ marketing/sales people can avoid considerable mutual frustration and wasted effort by proceeding slowly in reorienting the new entity to a broader view of its markets.

Building foreign sales can be accomplished in three ways: sending the acquiree's home office people on selling trips; establishing sales offices in other countries; or utilizing independent representatives in target countries. A combination of all three is possible, of course.

Which way to go can sometimes be decided at once by the product line. If the company sells aircraft instruments, there are only a handful of possible customers in all Europe, so visits from home office by salespeople and engineers may be sufficient.

For good results over time in most product lines, though, the best route is directly owned and operated sales offices whose people are local nationals. They speak the language, know all the local nuances, and live and work where their customers live and work, thus achieving optimum acceptance.

Establishing such offices is a difficult task, however, because of the shortage of qualified and willing people. Besides some technical knowledge of the products, certainly bilingual capability is needed, and willingness to represent a foreign company. Many an American company, rushing to establish sales offices in European countries, has come to expensive grief by setting up shop with the first people they could find, only to discover they were the wrong people. This has been coupled with the usual American impatience for concrete results, which frequently causes a foreign sales office to be closed too soon, even though the locally hired salespeople were right for the job and were making the correct moves to get themselves established with customers.

This leads to the conclusion that the U.S. parent's marketing people, after obtaining acceptance by the new subsidiary of a program to broaden its sales activities in other countries, should let the Europeans do the job themselves, in their own way.

In the personnel field, policies and practices with respect to operations in other countries will of necessity vary widely. You cannot simply apply compensation and benefit plans uniformly across the foreign operations, as you can with domestic divisions. The world headquarters people will have to be sensitive to the differing situations in different countries and flexible in their adaptations of overall corporate policies and practices to fit particular countries.

Example: when Harold Geneen set out to make the very loose confederation of companies that was ITT into an integrated multinational corporation, the New York headquarters people attempted at first to mandate a U.S. level of benefit programs across all subsidiaries in all countries Thus, when the large ITT Spanish company, SESA (Standard Electrico S.A.) presented their pension plan for headquarters review and approval, the then pension expert in New York rejected it immediately, because the plan called for paying retirees some 75 percent of their preretirement pay level. In the U.S., of course, 20 or 25 percent is more normal. The New York man failed to consider the hard fact that Spanish pay levels were so low that retirees would starve on only 25 percent of their working pay level. He also didn't take the time to find out what other Spanish companies did, which turned out to be pensions at the same level as SESA's proposal.

Another good example of what not to do with the new personnel was ITT requiring the European subsidiaries to begin using the full battery of U.S. aptitude tests on candidates for executive jobs. This program included also giving the tests to executives *already* in place. Imagine the furor! In addition to anyone's normal worry of tests perhaps exposing inadequacies, there was great fear of the unknown: such tests were hardly ever used in Europe at that time, and never used on executives who had been in top positions for years.

Besides the legitimate questions with respect to what was going to be done with the results of the tests, the level of emotional outrage was high: "You Americans have no right to dictate such nonsense to us," roared the chief executive of the big ITT German subsidiary, SEL (Standard Electric Lorenz). (Curiously, he himself was a firm believer in handwriting analysis, which was reqired for all SEL managers.)

The results of the tests? Predictably useless. They were in English, of course, with intentional language nuances beyond the grasp of many of the Europeans. They also contained references requiring a specifically American background to answer correctly, and so on. No use was ever made of the test results. So irritation, struggle, needless harassment of valuable people, and for nothing.

The moral is that headquarters people in a large multi-national corporation must think globally, and at the same time be flexible with respect to local situations. A lot of people, unfortunately, can't do this, or more likely, don't want to make the effort. It's much easier to be dogmatic at headquarters, and let some poor guy in the field struggle to keep the piece together. However, if an acquiring multi-national corporation wants to minimize internal friction and optimize performance, it must have broad-gauge headquarters people.

The acquired company's personnel will of course consist almost 100 percent of local nationals. There may be a few Belgians in a French company near the borders, and vice versa. Perhaps a Swede or two in a German company. An Englishman might pop up almost anywhere. But the vast majority will be local people, for all the reasons: language facility, national prejudices, the desire of most people to live in their home country among relatives and friends.

The new corporate parent should hesitate a long time before taking the initiative on inserting foreigners into the picture. Don't send a French accountant to the German company just because a position is open and the Frenchwoman is available from another subsidiary. Don't hire a German engineer for the Spanish factory, even though his qualifications fit the requirements. Let the local national company decide when and where foreign people are needed and can fit, and let them do the necessary searching and hiring.

When the acquired entity is an American corporation, but one that has international operations of its own, organization can be a considerable problem. How are international operations handled in the new parent corporation compared with the acquiree? If both use a worldwide product line or customer industry management, fine. But if one has worldwide product line management and the other is using an area management structure, such as North America, Europe, Asia, then obvious difficulties are present.

Worst is an area management corporation attempting to absorb an integrated company that is operating on a worldwide product management basis. The acquirer's European head will immediately lay claim to management responsibility for the acquiree's European operations, which have been reporting to a product line manager who may be located in Europe, but more probably in the United States. Ditto the area managers in the rest of the world. This produces discord everywhere. The acquired entity's European operations have been playing an understood part in a worldwide what-make-where/what-sell-where plan. Suddenly they are to report to a manager whose responsibilities are solely for Europe, and therefore considerably circumscribed and parochial, compared to the worldwide view. At the same time their former partners in the United States and Asia are now reporting to different area managers, all of whom will probably have different ideas as to the mission the acquired entity's operations in their territory should have.

My experience in international operations during most of my industrial career, seeing both area and product line managements tried many times, has led to the inescapable conclusion that worldwide product line management is better. Any corporation that is serious about participating worldwide in its product lines over the long haul had better have or develop worldwide product line management.

Otherwise, it will eventually lose out to competitors who do think, organize, and operate globally by product line. Of decisive importance, the product line management and profit and loss responsibility must coincide. Resolutely reject the various, perhaps glamorous-sounding but ineffective, hybrids.

ITT provides an instructive example. Harold Geneen installed area management shortly after becoming ITT president in 1959. Participating in his marathon monthly meetings in Europe from 1961 to 1964, I saw the evolution of his organizational thinking. Geneen very quickly grew impatient with numerous questions and problems that arose in Europe with respect to *other* areas in the world. One European company couldn't sell its communications gear in Latin America because, it said, the Latin America area sales effort was ineffective. Another objected to a U.S. ITT division selling its products in Europe through representatives in *competition* with its own equipment. A third asked why a particular long-range and expensive engineering program had gotten underway in a U.S. division when the European company was already working on the same project? You get the picture.

So Geneen, a quick learner, realized he needed a world product line approach, and he installed product line managers: at world headquarters in New York, at North American area headquarters, in Europe, the Far East, and Latin America—literally dozens of product line managers. *But,* the product line managers were installed in *parallel* with the existing company managements, who retained P & L responsibility. In addition, the area managements were *left in place,* fighting their area battles, jealous of territorial prerogatives, not really involved in the worldwhile success or failure of anything.

Not surprisingly, this remarkable mélange of crosscutting and undercutting responsibilities has proven ineffective. It is importantly responsible, I believe, for ITT's lackluster performance over the past decade. A mediocre record epitomized by the fact that ITT's stock price has remained virtually the same for the past eight years. Enormous expenditures of time and energy have been spent fighting internal battles rather than competitors.

Attempts are made to dignify these hybrid types of organization by calling them "matrix management," which means everybody is responsible. A beautiful example of an exercise in futility and self-deception.

But back to our integration problems. If the acquirer has area management and the acquiree product line management, then the organizational adjustment required is severe for the new entity. If that is the case, then move slowly in changing the reporting relationships. The acquired company was bought because it was doing well, usually not vice versa. Therefore, the parent corporation need not move hastily to disrupt existing patterns of product planning, what-make-where, and selling in the new entity. Rather take a careful look at just how important any jurisdictional problems or product overlaps really are. If they come down to only the egos of area managers being affected, then let the new entity be an anomaly in the corporate organizational structure. Perhaps then, as time passes and the top corporate people grow in wisdom, the superiority of worldwide product management will be recognized and the anomaly will be made the norm.

In the other case, where the acquiring corporation is enlightened and has effective product line management while the new entity is operating on an area basis, the adjustment is easier. This is because the president of the acquired company is usually really actiing as a worldwide product line manager, even though there may be area chiefs in Europe, Asia, and Latin America. The acquiree's chief executive will necessarily be pulling together the various strands around the world for making the basic what-make-where/what-sell-where decisions, with the advice and counsel, including conflicting opinions, of chief lieutenants.

Note that in the larger, acquiring corporation, the chief executive cannot do the integrating job necessary for all the corporate product lines. It is a task beyond the capability of any one person to do intelligently and effectively, though sadly some try from time to time, since the size of a corporate president's ego can be immense.

For the problems the international dimension introduces into other business functions, consider the acquired company's network of local connections: representatives and distributors selling the products, local lawyers and bankers and preferred suppliers—many of these relationships will be of long standing. The basic rule applies that changing or realigning these connections should be done slowly and carefully.

For example, if the U.S. headquarters marketing vice president insists on moving quickly in terminating some distributor relationships, because they may be handling products competitive to other divisions of the acquiring corporation, the damage monies that have to be paid to the affected distributors are large. This is because in many countries outside the United States, especially in Europe, one cannot simply terminate a distributor on short notice, as one can here, without incurring substantial financial liabilities.

If legal or outside auditor arrangements are changed quickly by the new parent, say to the firms in that country who are handling the corporation's other businesses, dire accusations, both subtle and direct, will be made by both the affected firms and their colleagues in the acquired company. The new parent corporation will be suspected of the most nefarious intentions. "The outside auditors are being changed so that the new ones can cook the books." "Our good lawyers are being dismissed so they can get ones more compliant for their schemes to avoid local taxation." So go slowly, and discuss patiently why some changes will be made, *before* taking action.

What else can be done to minimize these problems, besides having headquarters people who can think globally and give careful consideration and preparation before making changes?

Foremost is to keep the management people local nationals. Do not immediately insert an American or two anywhere in the top management structure. Twenty-five years ago this prohibition would have caused more trouble. Many business people outside the United States were accustomed to a more leisurely paced life then—less demanding performance criteria, less competitive environment—and many executives had no experience in conducting operations outside their own national boundaries. But today all that has changed, in considerable part because of the effect first of American companies, then of German, and more recently of Japanese, in extending competition across national borders, heightening awareness of the necessity of active and broad-gauged executives in the battle for survival, and forcing business planning on a worldwide scale.

As a result, first-class executives by any standard can now be found in all industrialized countries. National characteristics persist, of course. Your top man in Italy will be more vociferous and excitable than this Swedish counterpart. Your German manager will have more elaborate systems and procedures manuals than her English collegue. But they all can be first-class executives in any league, so use them, not Americans.

Next, the use of an ombudsman should be seriously considered. This person also must be a local national. An American would not be sufficiently trusted, at least at first. The local person will have this problem too, but in lesser degree. The job? The ombudsman would listen to worries, doubts, and suspicions of the new acquisition's people and discuss them with the executives of the parent who are responsible for the new entity. An ombudsman's comments and insights into what may be real concerns of the local people, as opposed to normal wailing in a newly acquired company, can be enlightening, and the suggestions useful.

At the beginning of this section was mentioned the "as often pretended as real" nationalistic feelings involved after an acquisition of a foreign company. This is an unpleasant area, but a fact of life to be recognized. In an international business this is the person who tries to enlist nationalistic feelings in his organization to support his favorite projects, or in opposition to those he dislikes. Fair consideration on the merits is not for this person; emotionalism and prejudice is his game.

"The big new engineering project had better be done here in Germany. Forget about doing it in the Italian company. Everybody knows Italian engineers are inferior." "The idea of manufacturing the new widgets in the Spanish factory to save labor costs is atrocious. Spanish quality control is nonexistent." "Our customers here in France won't buy a product from the German plant. Have you forgotten what they did to us in two world wars?" Add any other like comments you can imagine. They've all been used.

The best approach here is to be scrupulously fair-minded yourself, and to attempt resolutely to ignore the red herrings of prejudice thrown in your path. Keep the discussion on the track of seeking quantifiable, businesslike solutions to business problems. Set the good example of being above national prejudice, and you will find that the better people in the foreign operations will respond in kind. They, as do good business people everywhere, need people who are effective, regardless of age, sex, religion, or place of national origin. Support those managers, and ignore or eliminate the prejudiced troublemakers.

For all these reasons—language problems, personnel policy differences, nationality-based suspicions—even more time should be allowed, and more effort should be made, when integrating foreign subsidiaries. The headquarters people must be prepared to explain and explain again, to discuss, to defend corporate structure, policies, modus operandi, even more than when integrating a U.S. company. The time period required to integrate the functions of an acquired foreign company judiciously and effectively will be roughly double that needed for an American acquiree.

7

SYNERGISM RAMPANT

SYNERGISM—a good word, a good concept. The thinking is that, within a large, multi-division corporation, the whole can be greater than the sum of its parts. The various divisions will supplement each other's efforts and aid each other in diverse ways. Also, that the parent corporation's name should enhance the reputation of the individual divisions.

Because it seems such a good idea, quite rational, synergism is much cherished by corporate HQs. The staff tries hard to come up with cross-division practical applications of the theory: in product ideas, in manufacturing, in selling. Meanwhile the corporate advertising and publicity people want customers to *know* that Jerrold, the largest supplier of cable television equipment, is a division of General Instrument; that Pratt & Whitney, premier producer of jet engines, belongs to United Technologies; that the corporate parent of world processor manufacturer Vydec is Exxon. The recognition by customers of the corporate connection is intended to help the division sell product.

A good recent example of the synergistic hopes that are normal at large corporation headquarters is Allied Corporation, following its acquisition of Bendix. The Allied chairman explained that there were numerous synergistic possibilities from the merger. Allied's health-care unit might make use of sensors developed by Bendix aerospace. Allied's die casting division might fit with Bendix aerospace, or maybe the Bendix auto parts business. Bendix's military hardware businesses might utilize Allied's laser program.

Sound reasonable? Yes, but few such examples of top-level synergistic thinking actually are realized, and for good practical reasons that almost always defeat the synergism theory.

Each division of a large corporation is in a discrete business segment of its own. A division that is engineering, manufacturing, and selling electronic components lives in a different world from another division in the same corporation that makes small or large motors, or one making roofing materials, or one in the automobile rental business.

This is self-evident. What is equally true, though not obvious, is that besides wishing each other well as part of the same large family, there is little these divisions can really do to help each other succeed in their own separate business field.

Each division has to make its own way with its unique group of customers. To be successful, the division's special combination of product, price, service, and past record must appeal to those purchasers. A buyer obtaining motors from division a normally has no interest in the fact that division b of the same corporation makes electric typewriters.

The internal supply synergism ideas also run into difficulty. Allied's chairman says that its health-care unit might make use of Bendix sensors. Well, why aren't they using them now? Perhaps Bendix doesn't make the kind of sensors in which the health-care unit is interested. If they do make them, why isn't the Allied division buying? Price, delivery problems, maybe quality difficulty at some time or other—there could be any number of reasons. Maybe Bendix uses their sensors only internally, in equipment built for the military.

The base fact is that the health-care unit is not utilizing Bendix sensors. But now, following the merger, surely they will? Perhaps. Certainly the chairman mentioning the possibility will spur activity: at HQ, at Allied's health-care unit, and wherever in Bendix the sensors are produced. Questions will be asked, studies made, visitations will take place between the directly concerned Allied and Bendix people, with HQ staff following the proceedings.

Reasons why not to use will probably be as plentiful as reasons for Allied using the Bendix sensors. The type and sizes being made may not be suitable for the application. Considerable investment in engineering and tooling may have to be made by the Bendix unit to be able to supply what Allied health-care uses. The quantity needed by Allied is perhaps of no interest to the Bendix people when compared with their important customers' requirements. On such real-life rocks do many corporate synergistic ideas founder.

But can't Allied's chairman simply issue a "do it" order to the units involved? Of course he could, but he won't. Chairman Edward Hennessy is too realistic to force such actions from on high. He knows they could easily do much more harm than good.

The biggest staff temptation in synergistic thinking involves new product ideas. "How can we make $2 + 2 = 5$ through cross-division new product ideas? Division a makes electronic components, Division b, roofing materials. What can they do together to make the whole larger than the two parts?"

In due course a staff person comes in with a suggestion. "Let's make roofing materials with electronic sensor built in, which can be used to give alarm in case of fire on the roof." Why not? Memos go out to the roofing materials and the electronic component divisions. What do you think of the idea? Conduct market surveys, make product cost estimates, pricing guesses. How much time is needed for the engineering to be done? What investment in manufacturing equipment will have to be made? How big a market will there be?

People from the division are diverted from other tasks. Meetings are held between the two divisions. The work, which has to be done, of course detracts from the divisions' existing tasks. Since it is an HQ suggestion it can't, usually, be thrown out without a hearing, and without documentation on all the questions involved. If the interested staff person can get one of the top corporate executives to adopt the idea, the necessary effort to deal adequately with it increases greatly. The amount of time divisions have to spend on extracurricular activity of this sort is enormous in a large corporation.

The bigger the staff, the more such ideas will be floated. Another argument for a small HQ staff. This is not to say categorically that such synergism ideas from HQ people are always bad. Only that most of them are not worth the effort required to investigate, much less try to implement.

A GI synergism project in 1973 was hand-held calculators. The microelectronics division already made MOS (metal oxide silicon) chips. The Clare-Pendar division was making keyboards. The Signalite division was launching a miniature lighting display project for use in instrumentation. Thus the basic hand-held calculator components were being made in-house. Why not make the complete product? This was an HQ idea, of course.

Why not indeed? So for nine months the fur flew. For reasons having nothing to do with cost, the decision was made to assemble the calculators in a Canadian plant. The determining factor was that the plant needed work, and it quickly became apparent that the Canadians were the only division really interested in the project.

Microelectronics, struggling desperately at that time to find a niche in the computer-on-a-chip field, had numerous promising projects of their own, and they foresaw correctly that the prices for calculator chips would soon fall too low to be interesting for them. Clare-Pendar made large alpha-numeric keyboards for people like NCR, Datapoint, and Sperry Rand, which sold for $125 each. They didn't need a small $3 or less calculator keyboard among their other headaches.

Yet, because GI's president participated directly in the project, it acquired momentum and consumed a lot of talent and energy that would have been better utilized in the division's going businesses. However, as often in GI's history under President Frank Hickey, his practical nature asserted itself, nudged along by rapidly dropping calculator prices and red ink all over the project, and it was aborted before causing too much damage.

This story ended happily finally, in a triumph for the free enterprise system. Several hundred thousand of the by then too large, too costly, and outmoded GI calculators, along with the manufacturing equipment to make them, were sold to the Russians. Credit where due—the sale was negotiated primarily by the HQ vice president of marketing.

When the synergistic idea originates within a division, it has a better chance of success, if only because it is almost always more realistic than one from HQ. And the chance of success is enhanced if the relationship between divisions is simply that of a customer and a supplier. The division with the idea handles it like any new product of its own and deals with the sister division on an arms-length basis, just as it would with any vendor.

GI's Clare International in Belgium developed a telephone set that provided pushbutton action for older dial telephone instruments. It needed an MOS microchip, in addition to several relays that Clare already made. The Clare people first sought the necessary chips from GI Glenrothes, in Scotland. Although they were initially interested, it soon became clear that the Glenrothes people had bigger ventures to pursue. They were working on projects anticipating using several million chips a year, rather than the several hundred thousand that Clare could foresee. So Clare went to a non-GI chip supplier, Glenrothes went on about its business, and everybody was happy.

The point is that if an HQ staff person had suggested or been told to "coordinate" the project, disengaging Clare and Glenrothes would have been much more complicated and time consuming. The HQ person wanting synergism, would have urged the microchip people to do the project. Glenrothes would then have had to resort to the sadly time-honored techniques of seeming to cooperate while throwing sand in the gears.

The chip specifications would be discussed and debated endlessly. Samples of the chips would be delayed, design engineers pulled off the project because of "emergencies," prices quoted far above what Clare could afford to pay for its chips.

Eventually the outcome would be the same. Clare would go to another supplier, but meanwhile the project would be delayed, perhaps fatally, by the well-intentioned HQ interference, and Glenrothes would have suffered too, from diversion of engineering and sales time to an unwanted project.

Is the synergistic across-division new product project picture always gloomy? No. Where the corporate divisions are left free to treat with each others on normal seller-buyer terms, a lot of business is done within a corporation. At GI, the microelectronics operation supplies chips to the divisions making cable television equipment, keyboards, automatic wagering equipment, and point-of-sale computers. This does not happen by presidential fiat but because the product, price, and service are right as seen by the buyers, and the business is worthwhile as seen by the seller.

A different line of synergistic thought involves manufacturing facilities. One division possesses a first-class molding plant, producing plastic parts and housings for its own products. Other divisions in the corporation do not have molding capability, but they buy a lot of plastic parts from outside vendors. Why not have the molding plant supply the rest of the corporation's plastic parts needs? Get the cost-reducing benefits of larger-scale plastics molding operations. Keep the business in-house, benefiting the corporation overall. Enhance the esprit de corps between the corporation's divisions.

So the struggle begins. HQ informs all divisions of the well-meant objectives and urges them to start getting their plastic parts from their sister division. The design engineers, purchasing people, and manufacturers of the other divisions already have sources of supply, and they have been around the track of checking out potential new suppliers many times, so they proceed cautiously. They send the molding division their most difficult pieces, to look at and make samples for evaluation. Faced with a number of such hair-raising oddball parts from other divisions in the corporation, the molding operation wants to throw in the towel immediately.

"Look at this crazy stuff! Their engineers obviously don't know a thing about good plastic parts design. The tooling costs required even to make samples will be prohibitive. Anyway, I can't fool around with these requests and still handle our own projects." The molding plant manager is in high dudgeon, and with good reason.

The division general manager, however, wants to be a good corporate citizen: one for all and all for one. So she urges and cajoles until the molding man agrees to make samples of at least some of the requested parts. Greeted with dismay by the tool room, of course. Messy for the production people, since molding the samples will have to be crutched around going production activity.

Somehow the samples get done and are sent off, along with a preliminary price quotation. Of course both are greeted with derisive noises. "Your price is twice what we pay now. Did some sales guy's pencil slip or something?" say the purchasing people. "Look at this garbage," says the manufacturing man, "the tolerances are so wide that we'd have to throw away every other piece."

How much time and money is spent on such exercises within large corporations? The figures are astronomical, but it continues to be frequently tried because the dogma of synergism says there *must* be gold in those hills.

Another synergistic idea affecting manufacturing is that of having one production facility serve several divisions. That is, one factory to produce the products designed and sold by different divisions. This approach is worse than the "let's have one big molding facility," as shown by the answer to one question: To whom does the multi-division products factory manager report? The answer, sadly, is, to everyone. The manager is expected to be responsive to the needs of several division managers, an impossible assignment.

What actually happens is an interminable series of battles over what goes on in that factory: the way production is scheduled; how often those schedules can be changed; the priority of new product introductions or cost reduction programs; the allocation of overhead costs among the participating divisions; which division's products get the attention of the best people available at the plant. It is a very inefficient way to go and causes a lot of friction between the divisions. Avoid it.

At General Instrument in the early 1970s, the president endorsed the multi-division factory idea. There were to be several "corporate" plants, beginning with the very large one in Taiwan. This factory was already producing products for two or three divisions, but now its product spread was to be enlarged. The president added a new wrinkle to the basic idea that he hoped would avoid the negative aspects of multi-division factories: the corporate plans would not report to the division managers they served, but instead their plant managers would report directly to the president. Only the fact that President Hickey was himself a manufacturing man enabled this aberration to claim any respectability.

In practice the basic situation remained unchanged, that is, a continuing series of alarms and skirmishes went on between the corporate plant and the division users. Except that now the court of appeal had to be the president of the corporation himself. Reading the telexes that flowed into New York HQ at that time, all addressed to President Hickey, made one both laugh and cry. Division a was angrily informing the president that the plant in Taiwan was not meeting the required production rate. Taiwan fired back that shortage of piece parts that were supposed to come from the U.S. division made meeting the schedule impossible. Division b wanted to know when the plant was going to get off its duff and install the new quality control testing equipment that had been sent over. Taiwan asked in reply where the U.S. engineers were who were supposed to supervise the installation. All this back and forth, on numerous operating details, went directly to Hickey, frequently requesting or requiring his active intervention.

This "corporate plant" idea didn't last long at General Instrument. The president quickly found that he didn't need all those telexes to and from Taiwan cluttering up his desk. He had quite enough telexes to deal with on more important matters than adjudicating intramural squabbles. The exercise showed, though, how easy it is for a corporate HQ to overestimate what it can usefully do to help divisions in the day-to-day fray.

Combining sales operations is still another synergistic temptation for a large corporation's HQ staff. A look around gives a marketing staff person an idea. "We have Alpha division selling semiconductors, while

Beta division is selling relays. They're both electronic components, aren't they? Let's combine the two sales organizations and have just one group selling both semiconductors and relays. We then have our choice of using the doubled numbers of salespeople for greater market coverage, or saving money by cutting down the total number of salespeople."

On the surface this may seem reasonable. However, this is the sales analogy to the multi-product plant. The organizational problem is the same: to whom is the new merged sales organization going to report? If to the semiconductor sales manager, then relays will get the short end of the stick of sales attention. If to the relay sales manager, then vice versa.

But can't the sales manager of the merged organization, an intelligent, energetic man, be even-handed in how he allocates the sales effort among the two product lines? No—because breathing down his neck is the division manager to whom he reports, and that division GM is fiercely partisan about where he expects the sales organization to put its best effort.

Well, how about making the merged sales organization independent of both division managers? Let it report to the corporate vice president of marketing. Stop, this is the corporate plant situation all over again, only now deeply involving the top corporate marketing person in innumerable operating details for just two products out of the total corporate product/marketing responsibility.

Taking on such responsibilities, however, is a temptation to many vice presidents of marketing, because most of them do love to get directly involved in the selling effort. They believe, many times correctly, that no one down in the divisional selling activity can do a sales job as they can. Lucky the corporation, though, whose top marketing people resolutely keep out of the day-to-day selling effort at the divisional level.

A recurring theme when complicated organizational ideas present themselves is: "But with the right kind of people, can't even a complicated organizational set-up work OK?" Yes, it can, but those kinds of resolutely nonpartisan people are in as short supply in the business world as elsewhere. It is asking too much of almost everyone that they serve two or more masters equally well. All members of the organization need to know to whom they report, and what they are expected to accomplish. Matrix-style management approaches are a combination of fad and "let's dilute responsibility by sharing it" escapism. In effective corporations matrix management won't last long.

Or, If examined closely, what is called a matrix will turn out to have one top person who is making the difficult decision calls.

When a new acquisition enters the large corporate picture, what happens? Almost invariably there occurs a flurry of synergistic ideas at HQ. All the basic themes and variations are repeated. Joining the acquisition's capabilities with those of existing divisions to create new product lines are explored. Possible sales, engineering, and manufacturing combinations are discussed. An HQ staff person taking direct responsibility for a possible cross-division project is considered lovingly. All this activity is not to be condemned, either. The staff is just doing its job, looking for that elusive $2 + 2 = 5$.

How much actual impinging on the new divisional entity does take place will depend on the degree of maturity of the corporate top management and HQ staff. If the HQ players have been around the synergism track often enough to know the hazards from painful direct experience, all will be well. All the synergistic possibilities will be considered, yes. Indeed, they were, or should have been, explored before the acquisition was decided upon. But the corporate HQ will be very selective about how many ideas, and which ones, are actually raised with the acquisition's people. The ones that are will be introduced carefully, presented not as commands, but as possibilities that may be useful to the acquired division.

Where the acquiring corporation has too large a staff, looking for things to do and without enough experience with the cost and results of most cross-division synergistic projects, the acquisition is in for a rough and costly time. All sorts of trial balloon ideas will be tried out on the acquisition's people. Since the newcomers won't know how seriously to take these staff importunities, attention and effort will be diverted from the division's ongoing business. New studies will have to be undertaken, cost projections produced, visits to and conferences with other divisions of the corporation set up, perhaps customer surveys made. Almost all of this extra work, and attention of key people, will come to nothing, for all of the reasons discussed earlier.

The good answer is to spare the acquisition this kind of unwelcome diversion of effort from its existing businesses. Especially in the early months of its association with the new parent, when the nature of the staff/line relationships will be forming. To establish a good base, for lasting, mutually supportive rapport between HQ staff and the line division, a wise top management will not let synergistic efforts become rampant.

However, the synergistic possibility that will always be pursued by an HQ following an acquisition, is that of doing as much business internally as possible.

As soon as the acquired company comes into the fold, the top parent corporate management will want sister divisions to buy whatever products it markets from the acquired entity, and it will want the new division to reciprocate. The reasons are readily apparent. Doing business internally helps the corporation as a whole: additional sales volume accrues to supplying divisions, improving their margins and lowering costs; obviously, not using comparable products from competing corporations denies the enemy some business; corporate esprit de corps is helped by building mutual understanding and mutual sell/buy interdependence. All around a good thing for the corporation. Why then, does this area of internal sales cause so much irritation and grief?

Most corporations use one of three approaches for trying to control pricing transfers between their own divisions:

- Transfer at cost.
- Transfer at cost plus some percentage.
- Negotiate the price on an arm's-length basis, just as you would with a third-party buyer or seller.

The acquisition will have no trouble with the last item but will not like the first two at all, since usually it means it would have to accept a lower than market price for products sold internally.

Now, corporation presidents will seldom lay down an edict that where internal supply is available it must always be used, and absolutely forbid buying from outside suppliers. This is because most corporate presidents are realistic enough to understand that such an edict ties the hands of the buying divisions to a harmful extent. First, the in-house source may be unable to supply for some period for whatever reason, for example, manufacturing problems, strikes, problems with their own vendors. Then the corporation as a whole suffers more because of the absolute dependence of receiving divisions on the supplying division, when outside sources are absolutely excluded.

Second, with such an edict in place it is inevitable that the supplying divisions will treat the receiving divisions as second-class citizens. Without the discipline of having to be competitive with outside sources, the supplying divisions will simply not do as energetic and careful a job for the in-house user as they will with outside customers where competition is in the picture.

Most corporate presidents, accordingly, won't make buying in-house absolutely mandatory, but they will encourage it through policy statements and frequently try to regulate it as much as practicable by issuing an internal product transfer procedure, including transfer pricing.

The absolutely basic consideration is this: that both the supplying and receiving divisions must feel they are receiving a fair shake; that the supplying division couldn't receive a better price in selling to outside customers, or that the receiving division couldn't receive a better price or product by buying from an outside source. If both divisions are not satisfied that such is the case, then regardless of presidential exhortations and policy statements, they will not do business with each other.

If the buyer is not satisfied, quality and delivery problems will continually "occur." Products received will be judged unsatisfactory and will be sent back to the supplying division time after time; the purchasing department of the buying division will make impossible demands for delivery time; they will run the requirements up and down like the proverbial elevator; such as, "I have to have 1,000 pieces next week", and two days later, "Circumstances have changed. Don't ship me anything until next month." Wrangling over specifications with respect to quality, over testing procedures, etc., will consume horrendous amounts of time and energy. And if all else fails, the receiving division will actually sabotage the parts coming from the sister division in order to uphold their claim of quality problems. These are basic facts of life that cannot be ignored in considering this matter.

On the part of the supplying division people, if a mandated transfer price is judged by them to be too low for the effort required, then shipments will not be made on time, or in the right quantities. Outside customers will absolutely take priority at all times with respect to service, meeting extra requirements, etc., and the user division will be fed all kinds of excuses as to why the product is not forthcoming as promised and does not perform as advertised.

Haggling over price will go on interminably, whatever the transfer price policy says. If the policy says, "manufacturing costs plus 20 percent," how is manufacturing cost determined? Standard cost or actual? If standard is to be used, how current is it? If actual, how is the allocation of variances determined? I've seen mature people expending almost full time debating sister divisions' pricing. A sad waste.

Now consider transfers across national boundaries. A subsidiary in the United Kingdom is selling to one in the States. A U.S. division is selling to one in Germany.

To the problems already mentioned, add the troublesome items of different languages, national pride, suspicion of foreigners, and the already troubled waters become extremely agitated. Also, international transfers have further unique complicatioons, arising from theoretical, rather than realistic ideas about saving corporate money on import duties and local taxes.

In theory, a company will want to transfer a product between countries setting the transfer price low to save on import duties. In practice, however, this desire runs into considerations that severely limit the ability to lower transfer price just to avoid import duties.

First is the fact that the tax authorities in the country from which the transfer is being made will try to ensure that the supplying division is making a reasonable profit on the transferred product. It will be looking for a transfer price that is "reasonable," which usually means a market-level price.

Second, a reasonable average figure almost everywhere for components and equipment import duties is 10 percent. Thus, for each dollar of "price reduction" of transfer price in order to lower import duties at the other end, only $0.10 will be the duty reduction effect. This means that, to make the import duty saving large enough to be meaningful, a huge price reduction becomes necessary because of the 10–1 effect, and the supplying division would be left with a grotesquely low transfer price.

The subject of taxes, of course, always receives considerable attention. In theory, the multi-national corporation will want to make its highest margins in countries where taxes are lowest, and make its lowest margins in countries where taxes are highest.

If taxes are low in a country where the multi-national has a division that ships product to other divisions in other countries, then in theory, the transfer prices should be set high. If taxes are lower in a receiving country, then in theory the transfer prices should be set low for transfers from a division in a country where taxes are high.

In practice, however, these theoretical considerations run up against all the considerations mentioned earlier, where supplying divisions will simply find ways to do very little internal business if their margins, regardless of their local corporate tax rate, are not, to them, adequate for product shipped to a sister division. Similarly, a receiving division will buy very little from a supplying division if the transfer price because of tax considerations is set higher than prices for the same product from outside competitors.

The lesson in all the above is clear. Product transfers between divisions of the parent corporation, wherever located, should be made on an arm's-length, negotiated, competitive basis, the "normal" way to do business.

If the acquiring corporation is enlightened and operates this way, then the impact on the acquired company is minimal. If, however, there is a transfer policy in effect that requires internal transfers to be made at artificial price levels, then considerable trouble will result, Animosities, rather than esprit de corps, will be created, much time and energy will be wasted, and very little meaningful internal business will result. The hidden costs will certainly be greater than any apparent saving from a forced transfer policy.

An interesting aspect of transfers between sister divisions of a corporation remains to be discussed. What kind of selling effort should be made to sister divisions? Are they to be called on by sales personnel as an outside customer would be? Or can contacts between engineers and production personnel on both ends of the line do the job. Are the buying divisions people to be entertained, wined and dined, by the selling division? Or is this an unnecessary waste of corporate money? Thorny questions. But the answer becomes clear from consideration of the above points, or from experience.

As a young sales manager for General Electric's instrument transformer division, I was surprised early on that General Electric's own huge switch-gear division was buying some transformers from a competitor. In response to my query about this lack of corporate loyalty, the responsible switch-gear purchasing man stated baldly, "You never take me fishing on Chesapeake Bay."

General Instrument's Clare division lost business to outside competitors because its engineers didn't visit sister divisions with application or quality problems. How come? "Well, the pertinent manager said, "We are too busy taking care of *real* customers!"

The practical conclusion is that the internal division should be treated just as if it were an outside customer: including salespeople's attention, expense account wooing, the efforts of application and design engineers, and hand holding as needed by customer service and quality control people.

8
STAFF AND LINE
ENTREPRENEURS

PERHAPS SURPRISINGLY, the pioneering spirit manifests itself frequently in large multi-division corporations. Within the breast of many a staff and line person beats an eager entrepreneurial heart. Seeking to translate their ideas into action, their ambitions can lead the corporation into many an interesting venture, often far removed from its main lines of business. The result of those undertakings can be either success or failure, but they always produce turmoil and discord.

The entrepreneurial spirit in line divisions can certainly cause complications within a corporation. However, the effect of enterprising line personnel pales into insignificance when compared with the damage potential of ventures initiated by headquarters staff. These are almost always of more grandiose proportions, are less likely to succeed, and contain a larger personal ego component than "let's think big" projects initiated in line divisions.

The lower change of success arises from the simple fact that the staff people are farther removed from the product/customer battlefield than the deeply involved line division personnel. We all know the heady feeling that can arise when contemplating some project in the abstract, especially if it is one far removed from out daily duties. Well, that's the situation of the staff person, who sees the forest, not the individual trees. But while surveying that forest and dreaming of glory, one simply cannot appraise realistically the stubborn power of those trees. The trees that the line person runs into regularly: opposing, delaying, and all too often derailing even well-conceived ventures.

Staff-initiated programs also tend to be more ambitious in scale and promise grand results sooner, because the headquarters person promoting the idea is gloriously free from the restraints imposed by direct accountability for results. The line entrepreneur does have the prudence dictated by the responsibility of having to explain actual results vs. projections: why the costs are running way over target, why the venture is behind schedule, why those big customers' orders are so slow to appear. The staff person, in contrast, will be attending those review meetings and will be the one asking embarrassing questions. If the project idea was the staff person's, the theme vigorously pursued will be that the concept is flawless but implementation is obviously stumbling.

Finally, and not flattering to the character of the line people involved, a staff-initiated undertaking has less chance of success because of that old corporate problem—not invented here. Since the idea was thrown over the division transom by someone from headquarters, hackles immediately rise. After all, if it really is a good idea for the division, how come all those expensive folks in division management, or marketing, or engineering didn't think of it. Division credibility at corporate HQ depends chiefly on financial results, but also on the less tangible matter of being considered experts in their field. The division people, therefore, find it easy to be unenthusiastic about a project proposed by corporate staff.

Time and energy now have to be invested by important division people attempting to discredit the staff idea before it becomes a command. The division leaders point with alarm to the time of key people who would have to be diverted from the division's own projects; probable adverse effect on the division's profitability is overstated; customers are found who, asked the right questions, express disdain for the idea. The normal level of division complaints about headquarters interference rises in a crescendo.

But the true entrepreneur is not easily discouraged. The staff initiator lobbies for his idea, both at headquarters and with key division people. He urges the merits of his proposal with anyone he can get to sit still and listen. He writes strong memos lauding the merits of the venture. At planning meetings with the affected division, he raises the issue, forcing the participants to acknowledge and discuss it.

Within the division he pushes the proposal with some, but frequently little, finesse. He compares the projected excellent financial results of his idea with more modest division enterprises, asking, "Why do theirs when you can ring the bell louder with mine?" He may, regrettably, even indicate over a drink or two that his support of the division's pet projects is becoming contingent upon their picking up and implementing his idea.

Many such staff-initiated project ventures do fall by the wayside before reaching any active implementation stage. The staff man loses interest, perhaps because of the advent of an even more exciting quest he concocts. He may be switched to a different job with a new set of problems, or he may leave the corporation altogether. Some top executive may stop the enterprise cold with an early negative reaction. Corporate new product/new business priorities may shift, moving away from the area his venture addresses. Or the relevant division may be flying high, with rapid growth and good financial results. In such circumstances, a division can be much more cavalier in fending off, or bluntly rejecting, staff proposals.

Many, however, are eventually accepted, are built into a business plan, and implementation begins. Implementation begins—slowly and halfheartedly. Because the idea was not conceived locally, the "headquarters" project is a second-class citizen from the start. Division ventures take priority in any time or personnel crunch, or in budget restrictions. Worries about the worth of the project, and its current or potential difficulties, are magnified out of proportion. The division's best people in engineering and marketing are busy elsewhere.

The almost inevitable result: the project takes longer and costs more than any initial estimates. This is true, of course, for *any* project. But whereas a division-sponsored project on average will take twice as long and cost twice as much as forecast, any headquarters-imposed venture will double those numbers.

The upshot, therefore is that very few such enterprises come anywhere near producing the results joyously predicted by the staff entrepreneur months or years ago. He, however, is usually unaffected by the limping progress, or complete failure, of his brainchild. He can always say, and usually does, "Well, they didn't implement the idea properly," and many times he is absolutely right.

As you may expect, the higher in the corporate headquarters hierarchy that any entrepreneurial idea originates, the larger will be its scope, the greater its promised glories—and the farther from reality it will be. This reaches its zenith with chairmen and presidents of large corporations, and presents the ego factor in full flower. The best examples of monumental mistakes by mature, well-compensated top executives not surprisingly occur with acquisitions from fields foreign to the acquirer's own area of expertise.

Consider Xerox, father of the dry copier, a giant in its field, doing extremely well in the late 1960s. Too well, apparently, because Xerox's top management decided that the time had come to broaden the corporate activities into new fields. Perhaps copiers had become somewhat boring for the chief executives, too easy, though you can be sure they were not so for the line people toiling in the divisions. At any rate, hubris reigned at Xerox headquarters. What field did they decide to enter? Computers.

What was the matter with that? Nothing so far. If a Xerox division had proposed getting into computers, you can be sure the operating people involved would have started with a fairly modest target. Perhaps a small specialized computer, one for desk-top use. And the division proposal would not project quick, magnificent results. After all, by 1969 there were quite a few good companies competing in the computer field. Rushing in now could be quite hazardous.

But this was a corporate headquarters, top management idea, so the sky was the limit. The Xerox grand plan for computers was no less than to go head-to-head against IBM in the general-purpose computer market. Growing such a business from within was considered too slow and not certain enough to succeed. So acquisition of a company already in computers was decided upon.

But who good enough was willing to be acquired? Finally Xerox found a candidate. It was SDS, Scientific Data Systems, a California manufacturer of specialized computers used almost entirely in data acquisition systems for the aerospace industry. SDS was a good company, a leader in its field, but a long way indeed from IBM-type general-purpose business computers.

No matter, the Xerox chairman personally negotiated the acquisition and the terms were a stunner. Xerox, a 2 billion dollar sales giant, purchased SDS, doing 100 million dollars in sales, for 1 billion dollars. This was 10 times sales and 100 times SDS earnings, at a time when the going rate for acquisitions was between 10 and 20 times earnings.

But the stratospheric price was eminently justified, Xerox HQ maintained. Within five years, they proudly announced, they would be competing across the board with IBM via their SDS computer division. Seven years later both SDS and Xerox were out of the main-frame computer business altogether. The specialized scientific computer expertise of the SDS people proved insufficiently applicable to the general-purpose business computer market. Xerox was well over 1 billion dollars poorer, but, we can hope, wiser.

It is kind to draw a veil over the details of this debacle, but two morals are clear. First, when top managements launch into a monumental project, it had better be one in a product field in which they are knowledgeable. Second, no division entrepreneur, no matter how wild-eyed and visionary, could possibly cost a corporation as much as a chairman or president seized by entrepreneurial hubris.

Another good example is the largest acquisition in corporate history at the time it was made. This was General Electric paying a little over 2 billion dollars in 1976 for the acquisition of Utah International, a mining company. The intention was for GE to establish a solid position in the most popular buzzword field, namely energy, or natural resources. In that case the acquisition was at least deeply engaged in the selected field. No heroic launching of UI into other areas was contemplated.

Still, even though Utah International continued to do what it had been doing—mining—and GE top management knew that was the acquisitions's game, General Electric sold UI in 1983, only seven years later. Fortunately, unlike Xerox, whose billion dollars just disappeared, GE received 2.4 billion for its divestiture of Utah International.

The stated corporate reason for the divestiture was to utilize cash from the UI sale to enable General Electric to better focus its resources. OK, but why wait until 1983 to regain cash that could have been used to focus resources seven years ago? Why make such an acquisition at all? Clearly, in such cases, the top corporate general management and planners go wrong, launching mammoth projects that are must better avoided in favor of doing better what the corporation already does well.

Consider another monster acquisition, Exxon's buying Reliance Electric in 1974. Energy was the theme, specifically energy conservation. Admittedly, 1974 was a bad time for lucid thinking on the part of oil companies, battered as they were by the Arab countries' oil embargo, but even so. . . .

At the news conference announcing Reliance's absorption by Exxon, the giant oil company's chairman held up a small electrical device. He solemnly assured his audience that they were looking at the realization of a revolutionary new idea for motors. Now with Exxon's financial backing, Reliance would proceed to mass production of this powerful little baby, whose unique new design would save America millions of watt-hours of energy through making motors more efficient.

Yet today, nine years later, there is no sign of any revolutionary device such as was so proudly heralded at the time Reliance entered the Exxon fold. Apparently even Exxon's financial muscle couldn't generate the necessary invention. And, sadly, it is widely acknowledged that Exxon has not been pleased with the performance of its acquisition.

It would be interesting to know what went on between Exxon's chairman and his opposite number at Reliance with reference to the new idea before the acquisition was consummated. Did the oil man know enough about motors? Probably not, but among his large staff is surely a good motor expert? No? Then how about outside consultants being used to check on the motor's possibilities? They were, and Booz, Allen, Hamilton was enthusiastic about the potential of Reliance's new idea. So Exxon's top management, oil men, accepted at face value the Reliance and consultants appraisal.

But would Reliance, well known in its field and highly diversified in the electrical equipment industry, tell fibs about its development projects in order to encourage an acquirer? Outright fibs, no, but putting the best face possible on its activities, yes. An enthusiastic development engineer can make blue-sky projects sound very close to realization, especially when the listeners do not know the technology under discussion.

The preceding examples involved billion dollar acquisitions, but the companies making them, fortunately for shareholders, had the financial wherewithal to survive the grand entrepreneurial initiatives from the top that went sour. But the chairman or president ego syndrome can be so extreme as to actually lead to "betting the company" on one roll of the dice. Example: Bendix.

The Bendix–Martin Marietta fiasco of 1982 stands as a monument to executive hubris. Bendix, with 4 billion dollars in sales, was no small potatoes in the diversified large corporation lineup. Yet its chairman, who had enjoyed a meteoric rise from an originally financial background, dreamed of an even larger empire. The route: acquisition. The candidate: Martin Marietta, which at 3½ billion dollars in sales was almost as big as Bendix.

The Bendix chairman made friendly overtures, only to find that he was dealing with egos as big as his own. "If there is going to be any acquiring, we'll do it," was the message from Martin Marietta's top people, "Go away and leave us alone." Thus rebuffed, the Bendix chairman escalated to an unfriendly takeover bid, and the war was on. Martin Marietta countered with their own bit to buy Bendix, and the situation went from bad to terrible. Both corporations bid up each other's shares to twice their previous levels in a frantic battle to buy control, thereby saddling their balance sheets with huge new and unnecessary debts.

When the smoke finally cleared, Martin Marietta had precariously maintained its independence; the initiator of the battle, Bendix, was now owned by Allied Corporation, and the "bet your company" former chairman of Bendix was out of a job.

Are corporate headquarters entrepreneurial efforts always failures? No, but actual results, as opposed to original expectations, show a definitely higher mortality rate than for ideas originating in line divisions. This is especially so if the new business venture is one outside the scope of the corporation's current activities.

Du Pont's 1980 acquisition of Conoco was a corporate HQ step that meets the test of logic, even though it will be a business generation or two before the returns are in on its real success or failure. A chemical company like Du Pont, it is true, doesn't know a lot about oil exploration or refining, but it uses in great volume the products of that industry. Oil-based chemicals are an essential part of a chemical company's plastic products. So Du Pont wasn't interested in being in the oil business per se. It wanted an assured supply of refinery oil that is usable in Du Pont plastics products, and they got it in Conoco.

Or consider Philips of Holland, one of the world leaders in consumer electronic products, lighting, electronic components, and telecommunications equipment, especially in Europe. Philips has been growing rapidly in the United States, primarily through acquisitions.

It has bought Westinghouse's lighting operations, Sylvania and Philco consumer products businesses, the consumer electronics activities of Magnavox. Philips has also acquired Signetics, a semiconductor manufacturer, and had entered into joint ventures with Intel, Du Pont, and Honeywell.

But all these acquired businesses and joint ventures fit neatly into the main lines of activity of Philips. They are in product areas where the acquiring corporation is already strong and knowledgeable. This is adding strength to strength, promising success much more logically than acquisition of businesses far removed from those a corporation knows well.

Smaller corporations seem to have more success than the giants in entering new business fields on headquarters initiatives. This is because the smaller corporation top managers are closer to their businesses, and to the lower level processes of business, than the multi-billion dollar corporation president. The giant corporation head is buffered almost totally from the stresses and indignities that are the normal lot of the smaller company top person, who has frequently to deal directly with irate customers, recalcitrant suppliers, and prima donna employees. These experiences keep the smaller corporate president's feet on the ground, induce caution, and even engender some degree of humility, a useful offset to overenthusiastic hubris.

A newly acquired company, now a division, gets introduced to the staff entrepreneur problem sooner or later. Sooner, if the new entity's business is one closely related to other product areas of the corporation. Or if the acquisition was made with a definite eye to new projects, thought important, that the new division could undertake. Later, if the acquisition's businesses are new to the staff people. In that case, headquarters entrepreneurs will circle warily for awhile, unsure how the acquisition could best fit into implementation of brilliant ideas.

The predictable reaction of the acquired company to the first overtures by an enterprising staff person is negative. "We're very busy doing our own things. Have a full plate of exciting new projects of our own. Can't possibly consider it now." Further, being new to the corporation, the acquisition's people will violate unwritten taboos. They will ask questions like, "Who is going to pay for this? Do you have some spare engineers at HQ who can come out here to do the job? Whose financial statement gets affected if it doesn't fly?"

Looking suitably pained at such gauche utterances, the staff person admits that it's just a thought for consideration. "Of course if you do undertake such a project, it becomes entirely your division's responsibility. Naturally I'll be available for advice and counsel if you so wish. And give it a look, it just might be a winner."

The new division's people are in a no-win situation. Adding the suggested project to their existing load ipso facto detracts from current endeavors and costs money, with a negative impact on their profitability, which even now is being scrutinized intently by the top management and the HQ financial people. Ignoring the recommended project creates a possibly hostile HQ person, who won't be slow to pounce on future faults and failings of the new people.

What to do? Ameliorating the situation has to begin at HQ, with the management. No corporate president wants to stifle creative thinking among staff people—just the opposite. The president *wants* to encourage entrepreneurial impulses in both staff people and line personnel and hopes some of them will be successful. So the answer is certainly not a blanket rule forbidding staff people to present and lobby for product projects of their own that they consider valuable.

Aiding, yet reasonably controlling, staff activity with line divisions on behalf of HQ-initiated ventures depends on two key elements:

First, allowing only such initiatives as are approved by top management to be presented to the divisions; and second, allowing the divisions to recognize the cost of committing necessary resources in their business plans and budgets, and making allowance for the resulting negative P & L effect when reviewing their financial operating results.

The gateway review for all such HQ staff suggestions should be made by the planning vice president, assisted by the vice presidents of marketing, engineering, and manufacturing. These top-level executives are best qualified to rate the suggested projects in the context of all the corporation's business plans, and assign them a priority in competition with the other new ventures the divisions are already engaged in or are considering.

There then needs to be sufficient time allowed for careful review of the project by the division or division involved. The comments on, and evaluation of, the HQ idea by the line people who will have to implement it deserve serious consideration by corporate management. It's the forest and the trees again. Ideas that sound good in the far-from-the-fray atmosphere of headquarters may have definite practical difficulties connected with them. The line people directly involved in the specific business area targeted by the staff idea are in the best position to see and warn of potential pitfalls.

A competent top corporate management, whose members have come up through operating divisions themselves, will be able to separate the wheat from the chaff in the division worries and objections. Standard protests boil down to "We're too busy," "Not invented here," and "We can't afford it," and can be gently but firmly pushed aside. Attention then can be focused on real difficulties; for example, the technical competence available in the division may simply not be up to the requirements of the project, or, unknown to the staff person, two other companies may already be in the field with a similar product.

This three-step approach—HQ top management review of the staff-proposed project, division review and presentation of capability and problem areas, then top management re-review—can weed out most of the ideas whose attempted implementation would be a mistake. Then, if the decision is to proceed, the implementing divisions may not be overjoyed, but they will have had a fair hearing, so will go to work in much better heart than if the HQ idea had been forced down their throats.

Turning to consideration of entrepreneurial souls in the divisions, a frequent sore point within corporations, and the subject of longstanding debate, is the inevitable tension and guerrilla warfare between activists in the division and the HQ staff watchdogs.

The venturesome division person sees the conflict as a stifling of individual initiative by plodding, unimaginative HQ people. The staff person sees it as incessant attempts by wild-eyed division types to launch costly schemes that have only a remote chance of success.

The "official" time for debating the merits of new product ventures, retooling and reequipping factories, and expanding capacity is during the business planning cycle. The business plan document from each division, if well done, will state how the engineering monies and investment capital included in the plan will be spent; what new product projects will be launched or completed; and what financial and market share results are expected from them. At headquarters, the staff has the responsibility to sift through all the proposals from all the divisions and give them a priority ranking. Most often, the hopeful ideas for projects greatly exceed the available corporate resources.

Of course there is a built-in restraint in the divisions' plans, and that is the general market and financial picture expected. New business plans are not drawn up in a vacuum. For existing divisions, there is history, continuity, past performance, and expectations that exist at both the HQ and the divisions.

A business unit that is doing $50 million in sales and spending $5 million per year on engineering is unlikely suddenly to present a plan showing $100 million in sales for the very next fiscal year, along with $10 million in engineering expenditures. No, the changes usually included in business plans for the next year or two are incremental ones. Sales go up or down 7 percent, or 10 percent. Engineering expenses go up 10 percent. The first year or two out in a business plan can arouse a lot of discussion, but the changes from historic levels, and from this year, are seldom startling.

The situation is different, of course, for any completely new business ventures the corporation may launch. In such cases, the newly assigned division top management team is given dollars, people, and equipment resources, and told, "Make this idea a reality." The business plan produced by such a new enterprise may well show jumps of hundreds of percent in both sales and expenses in each of the first several years. But this is because they are starting from zero.

For long-existing divisions, dramatic year-to-year changes are seldom seen in a business plan (they very often occur in reality, however, but that is a different subject).

It is in the farther out years of a business plan that dramatic changes occur, say in the fourth and fifth year of a five-year plan. And here is where the staff/line conflict occurs. A division put $250,000 of engineering money in their plan for next year, for zero sales of promising new product. But in the fifth year of the plan, that new product is shown as producing $10 million of sales, earning 20 percent net after taxes, and returning 40 percent on investment.

Who can resist this? Well, the staff can. They've seen dozens of these potential gold mines before and their hearts have been broken many times by failures of highly touted projects. So they question the project intensively. They infuriate the eager division people with multiple criticisms. They doubt the world is waiting for such a product. Alternatively, they think the Japanese will do it sooner and better. They want more documentation on the market and on the proposed design. They question the projected costs, the expected pricing, the forecast volume. They compare the project unfavorably with many other, more worthy projects included in other divisions' plans. They cruelly mention past failures on the part of that division. They dwell lovingly on previous staff warnings disregarded, with resulting disasters.

The division people fight back. They cite earlier successes. They remark, frequently with colorful language, on the inability of the staff people to judge correctly the merits of the proposed project. They warn of competitors getting a head start in a promising new field, of dissatisfied customers, of loss of market position, of eventual financial disaster if the proposed venture is thrown out.

Eventually the president, or whoever is chairing the business planning meeting, halts the discussion, which is a complete standoff, and renders a decision, or postpones making one.

The division retires, happy with an OK, concerned about a postponement, muttering mutinously if the decision is, "Drop it!"

Being red-blooded people, however, the divisions don't take "drop it!" as final. So now begins the corporate games playing that wastes so much time and energy. What does the division do? It goes underground with its project. There is diversion of engineering time and money from other projects; or their total engineering expenses just happen to run $250,000 over budget; or they retitle and rework the project, presenting it again in a new costume or as a desperately needed "ex-budget" enterprise.

When Harold Geneen became president of ITT, he found two large projects involving computers in his European companies. One was a joint venture of the subsidiaries Standard Electric Lorenz (SEL) of Germany and Le Matériel Téléphonique (LMT) of France. They had taken a very large contract from Air France to produce a computerized flight reservations system. This was 1960, and such computerized systems were in their infancy. The other enterprise was a large time-sharing computer that had been built by ITT's Standard Telephone & Cables (STC) in England. Two such computers had been built, with the first one put into operation in London.

Both projects, being pioneering efforts in their fields, had run into the usual problems: time to complete was much longer than expected, and cost overruns were well beyond any forecasts. Air France was threatening cancellation with exorbitant penalties, and few customers were appearing for the time-sharing computer in London, an idea ahead of its time.

After watching these undertakings limp along, dripping red ink with every step, Geneen laid down the law. No ITT company was to get involved in any project involving the engineering and manufacture of a computer. Period.

But the lifeblood of ITT's European subsidiaries was telecommunications equipment, which they manufactured for the telephone administrations in every Western European country. And— here's the point—these administrations were all starting to go to computer-controlled central switching systems for their new equipment purchases. The European ITT subsidiaries *had* to get involved in engineering and manufacture of computers if they were going to stay in their best business, telecommunications equipment.

The European general managers tried to explain the necessity of involvement in computers to Geneen, at first in vain. I remember asking

Dr. Maurice Delorain, urbane head of the ITT French companies, "Why can't you talk sense to Geneen about this?" "Mr. Geneen," he replied, "is a man who must be educated little by little, otherwise he explodes too soon."

The entrepreneurial spirit, as well as a healthy sense of self-preservation, took over in the ITT European companies. Their computer-controlled switching system programs went underground. The first one to be completed was built by ITT's Bell Telephone Manufacturing (BTM) of Belgium. Made for the Norwegian telephone company, this system was the first large European programmable computer-controlled telecommunications switching system. However, in the descriptive literature for the system, the word "computer" never appeared. The equipment was simply described as a "fully electronic" switching system. In this case the entrepreneurs won, fortunately for ITT.

By the mid-1960s Geneen had become fully aware of the critical nature for ITT of the convergence of computers and telecommunications switching systems, and presto, computer-controlled system projects popped up from underground all over ITT's Europe.

A similar situation with respect to computers, but with a different outcome, arose in General Electric in the mid-1950s. Remember that at the time the future of computers in business use was still problematic. IBM was just a shadow of its present giant self.

General Electric set up a new division in Phoenix, Arizona, to get the company into computers. Talent was assigned to the division and funds were allocated. The computer people wanted to design and market computers for general business use, seeing the potentially high growth in such a market.

However, Ralph Cordiner, GE's president, had a different idea. He felt that computer use in manufacturing process control applications was the real future for General Electric, not general business activities. This was because General Electric was the leader in electrical equipment control of manufacturing processes in the United States. So Cordiner ruled that GE's new computer division would focus on manufacturing process control, not general business applications.

But the Phoenix organization was well along with the design of a computer for business use, specifically for banking transactions, intended for Bank of America. The Computer was finished and installed, one of the first general purpose computers used in banking.

Unfortunately for General Electric it was also that last, as headquarters insisted, and made it stick, that the Phoenix computer division restrict itself to computers for manufacturing process control applications.

The GE computer division entrepreneurs lost that one, and today IBM, in the computer business alone, is bigger than all of General Electric's 1,001 businesses put together.

There's a postscript to the General Electric story. It illustrates the fact that when a corporation misses out on a big new market in which it could have been a significant factor, the opportunity just does not recur. In the mid-1960s GE bought half of Machines Bull, the government-backed French computer manufacturer, intending to give the general purpose computer field a good second try. But by this time, of course, IBM, NCR, Control Data, Burroughs, and others were far down the road. The result, ten years and many millions of dollars later, General Electric finally decided to cut its computer business losses and sold its interest in Bull to Honeywell.

Sometimes perfectly reasonable corporate circumstances conspire to foil or delay implementation of a line entrepreneur's bright idea. Such a case in General Instrument was the story of light emitting diodes (LEDs).

These colorful little beauties were in their infancy in 1970, having just emerged from Monsanto's laboratories. But on the horizon, for the perceptive observer, loomed extraordinary growth possibilities. LEDs for hand-held calculators turned out to be the first of the big markets, followed by instrumentation of all sorts, from space shuttles to automobiles.

General Instrument's line manager of its miniature lamp business wanted the corporation to get in on the ground floor of LEDs, and it could have been done. GI had the talent, access to markets, a good name in tiny light sources. But the corporation had much more pressing needs for the available financial resources, which in 1970 were slim. So an LED program was out at that time.

Three years later, the corporation was booming, money was available, and top management gave the "go" sign for light-emitting diodes. The implementation task was assigned to GI's semiconductor division rather than the miniature lamp people. This was on the sound ground that making LEDs is much more similar to producing semiconductors than to making incandescent lamps, but also for the more dubious reason that the semiconductor division promised much faster and more glorious results than the lamp division would forecast.

Regrettably, General Instrument was soundly beaten by the competition. By 1973, Monsanto, Hewlett-Packard, General Electric, and several smaller but good companies were dominating the field. General Instrument started and remained an also-ran. By 1976, the semiconductor division decided it had bigger fish to fry elsewhere, and the LED hot potato was handed back to the lamp people.

The lamp division felt that by this time the only realistic chance for General Instrument to become an important factor in LEDs, without prohibitive cost, was via an acquisition. We zeroed in on one of three leaders, Monsanto, believing that a large chemical company could well become uncomfortable with an electronic components business like light-emitting diodes. And so it turned out, Monsanto, responding to our overtures in 1978, expressed willingness to divest its LED division.

The acquisition took much too long to consummate but was finally completed in 1980. Thus, ten years after the initial entrepreneurial proposal, General Instrument was finally in the light-emitting diode field in a big way.

Good entrepreneurial ventures promising real success can sometimes be killed within the division where they originate because of lack of local management understanding. Corporate headquarters isn't the only ogre in the enterprising division person's world.

Such a case occurred in General Electric's meter and instrument division. The principal product was watt-hour meters for electric utility use. But during World War II, the building of watt-hour meters was severely restricted because critical materials were being devoted to the war effort. Remarkably enough, the division's instrument people then came to the fore, and, through brilliant engineering, secured a place for GE in aircraft instruments for military use.

That GE division came out of the war with its aircraft instrument business almost equal in size to the prewar mainstay, watt-hour meters. So the future should have been bright indeed, with the division now possessing two main product lines instead of one. But no, division management, old watt-hour meter hands, returned happily to churning out millions of meters, and the aircraft instrument business was killed.

The method of execution was the internal costing procedure, specifically allocation of overhead. At budget time, the percentage of direct material and labor cost that was to be added to cover overhead expenses was determined by watt-hour meter standards. These were fixed on the basis of fairly closely determinable estimates of expected sales volume. But the aircraft instrument business could have a wildly fluctuating percentage of direct cost needed to cover overhead, depending on the size of contracts secured.

The aircraft instrument people pleaded in vain for division management understanding of the situation, pointing out that a 50 million dollar contract obtained would reduce dramatically their overhead cost per unit. But no, watt-hour meter standard overhead percentages had to be applied to every aircraft instrument cost estimate, making their bids noncompetitive on large contracts. Within a few years, General Electric's aircraft instrument business had shrunk to a shadow of its former self.

Now consider any acquisition coming into a large multi-division corporation, and the effect of its entrepreneurial spirit. The previously independent company has from time to time launched unusual new product ventures, sometimes remarkably far removed from its main line of business. As examples: a telecommunications equipment company getting, successfully, into the manufacture of commercial refrigeration equipment; an instrument company making golf carts; an electronic components company making miniature racing cars.

What is going on here? Sometimes the far-out new product is a pet idea of a company president or vice president. But always the proposals have come from within the organization, and almost always there is a known tie-in between the company and the intended market.

The amount of serious attention that such offbeat new product ideas receive in the new corporate parent's headquarters depends on a number of factors. For the formerly independent company, however, the very important psychological factor was that the decision whether or not to proceed could be made locally. It therefore jolts the acquisition's people to discover that from now on they cannot push off on totally new product enterprises without lengthy headquarters review.

What is needed from the new parent, to minimize the irritation of the new restraints, is first, careful consideration of the entrepreneurial projects that are already under way in the acquired entity. They should not receive a hasty review followed by immediate rejection, even though they are far outside the new division's main business lines. Few of them will prove to be matters of life or death, certainly not for the parent corporation, and very seldom for the acquisition, either.

As for new ideas that are just being floated, these can be considered as part of the normal business planning and budgeting cycle. Not peremptorily dismissed as not in the approved product range of the acquisition. This deliberate and thoughtful approach by the headquarters people to the entrepreneurial spirit in the new division will be a helpful step toward creating good will between acquirer and acquiree.

9

BUSINESS PLANNING

BUSINESS PLANNING in any corporation is as onerous as it is necessary. Necessary because a blueprint or road map of where the corporation is trying to go, and how it proposes to get there, is clearly a basic requirement. But why so onerous?

The basics of business planning are simple: Here are my resources; here is what I propose to accomplish with those resources; and these are the milestones I will use to monitor progress toward the goals. Business planning cannot just consist of the goals. It must encompass specific actions that will get the company from where it is to the goals.

Unfortunately, the planning does not take place against an orderly backdrop. The scene shifts continually. Competitors are active; customers changes general business conditions don't remain stable very long—they are always moving up or, much worse, down. And there's the rub. Priorities that seem reasonably clear this month change next month. Internal battles, or differences of emphasis, of opinion, pile on top of the external problematic situations. The entire planning process, which must be an ongoing one, that is, throughout the year, take place in an atmosphere of uncertainty, of conflict.

These are the reasons why business planning is onerous, why people don't like to do it. Internal conflicts, differences of opinion, must be tackled and resolved. Is the new product x more important than retooling the existing plant, when capital funds are limited? Will a competitor's new product y make much of an impact on existing sales? Marketing thinks it will, engineering brushes it off as inferior to the company's own equivalent product. Finance, whose contribution to business planning is all too often just the litany, "Let's remember we're in business to make a profit," may actually come up with an idea. The controller proposes stopping any further product modifications on older product line a in order to put more funds into promising new product b. Marketing objects because several good customers are even now asking for a new style of the older product. And all of this has to be eventually reduced to numbers and expressed in P & L statements, balance sheets, and cash flow.

The degree of difficulty involved is illustrated by the history of formal business planning in large, even well-disciplined corporations following its formal introduction.

I was with General Electric in 1952, the year President Ralph Cordiner introduced formal business planning in a detailed way, that is, at the division level. Prior to that, forecasts of GE's probable financial results in ensuing years were developed by a handful of people at corporate HQ in New York. Putting the task at division level obviously now involved thousands of people. Equally obvious was the fact that a great many of the responsible people at the divisions didn't like the idea at all. After all, to put into writing your expected financial results and plans for producing those results represents a kind of commitment, doesn't it? What if the plans are not met—not through your fault, mind you, but because of a whole host of external factors? Heads might roll, blots appear on the record, promising careers be blighted. No wonder a lot of people, including division general managers, tried to stay as far away as possible from the first plans produced.

"What business plan? Oh that, I've never seen it. Had nothing to do with it. It said what? Crazy. Well you know it was made up by a couple of clerks in accounting." Or, "Of course I knew about the plan. It was done all wrong in the first place. I could have kept them from making all those mistakes, but they didn't ask me the right questions."

The "we'd rather pass" school was aided greatly when President Cordiner stated publicly that he expected General Electric growth of 7 percent per year over the next five years. Eureka! Happy general managers summoned their financial men and instructed them to prepare financial projections showing growth of 7 percent per year for each year of the five-year business plans. No problem.

Obviously Ralph Cordiner had in mind a more careful division-by-division evaluation of their *individual* prospects. So when the next year rolled around and his intentions were made bitingly clear, the recalcitrants shifted to another tack. "How can we, low on the totem pole division people, know what direction the economy is going to take, and without that how can we forecast?" Corporate headquarters' guidance was needed, they pleaded.

General Electric then put in place a group of economists at headquarters who produced a volume of expected economic factors to be taken into account in preparing the next business plans. When these books were received, division people eagerly thumbed through them to get the magic word with respect to their specific product lines. Of course they were disappointed. The turbine people wanted to see a forecast of just how many turbines would be bought each year, and of what sizes. The headquarters economic forecast predicted that U.S. consumption of electrical energy would grow 10 percent per year. The jet engine people wanted to see how many military jet engines were going to be bought, and by what aircraft manufacturers. The headquarters forecast predicted a rising level of government defense expenditures.

Questions and recriminations flew back and forth, and by the time Cordiner again made clear that each division had to be responsible for its own specific forecasts, another planning year had gone by.

The next defense of the anti–business plan constituency, and it was numerous, was to change from saying, "We don't want to do it" to "We don't know how to do it." A variant was a plaintive "If only we really knew what headquarters wants, we could produce some really dandy plans."

This had two results. First, the headquarters instructions for preparing a plan grew rapidly from being chiefly a set of financial exhibits to become a book-length exposition of $2 + 2 = 4$: "If your market is $100 million, and you are doing $25 million in sales, then your share of market is 25 percent." Or, "It is important to know who your best customers are, and if they will be buying more or less next year." The second result was Cordiner's decision that each division was to have a new type of executive, a business planning manager, on the same level as the division functional managers of marketing, engineering, manufacturing, finance, and personnel.

The anti-forces began puzzling over the $2 + 2 = 4$ instructions, finding them quite complex, but they immediately recognized the new business planning manager as a bonanza. "OK, we've hired the guy, now he'll do the business plan," and they walked away from whatever was produced. It was his plan, not theirs. To end this recital, it took a good five years in General Electric, a well-disciplined company, finally to make business planning meaningful and not just cosmetic.

In 1960, Harold Geneen introduced formal business planning to ITT, shortly after becoming president. Because of GE's pioneering effort and a steadily increasing number of large corporations struggling to implement meaningful division-by-division planning, much of the spadework had been done.

The "why bother?" school within ITT, however, was given powerful support by Geneen's superdogmatic approach. His instructions were unequivocal. "There are to be no down years shown in any division's plans. Every year must be up. Further, every quarter of every year must be up at least 10 percent from the same quarter of the preceding year."

Did this approach produce realistic, meaningful plans? No. Did it produce a large number of ITT executives skilled in doublespeak, avoidance of responsibility, fighting each other for survival in an Alice-in-Wonderland atmosphere? Yes. After one down year, division managers were out. Since down years *will* occur, the turnover of ITT general managers all through the 1960s was one of the highest ever in a large corporation in American industrial history.

A final example of the evolution of corporate business planning. In the late 1960s General Instrument's then president, Monty Shapiro, completed his remarkable series of first-class acquisitions. He then strove to implement meaningful divisional business planning. This effort was brought to fruition in the 1970s under Frank Hickey, Shapiro's successor as president and chairman.

Hickey's approach was pragmatic. He wanted realistic plans. Up, of course, if at all reasonable, but a down year could be spelled out in a plan if necessary. And, importantly, submittal of such a plan did not require the simultaneous resignation of the responsible division manager.

Hickey's attitude fostered the kind of open and frank discussion of business plans that is essential to corporate progress and even survival in today's business world. Not that GI division plans projecting mediocre results or a down year were accepted without objection. President Hickey conducts *loud* planning meetings: assumptions are vigorously debated; suggestions for improvement are pressed hard; sarcasm concerning lack of managerial competence or imagination is ladled out lavishly. Still, when all is over, general managers at GI have been given a fair hearing and end up with a challenging business plan, but not one that requires supernatural intervention to be achieved.

With this background, let's now look at the problems of business planning when integrating a newly acquired company into a larger corporation.

Today, relatively few companies of any size do no business planning at all. The number of rugged individualists who disdain any formal business planning is getting smaller all the time. The ones who are left are usually the entrepreneurs who founded the business and guided its growth. And although they don't make up a nice plan book, you can be sure they are doing planning mentally all the time. *They* can afford not to commit to paper because they know the business from the ground up, and because they don't have to explain their plans to anyone.

Many more companies have a written business plan, but it is usually nowhere near as specific, as detailed, as those of the larger multi-division corporations. A good five-year business plan for a division today in ITT, General Instrument, or General Electric will consist of some two hundred large pages: about half-and-half text and financial or other exhibits.

To a newly acquired small company, the sight of what is expected in the way of a formal plan is often a nasty shock: disbelief mingled with concern, and with a few raucous horse laughs thrown in.

In some ways it is easier if the new subsidiary has not had a detailed planning system of its own. In such cases there is not the necessity to learn new planning language. The acquiring corporation has a planning philosophy and methodology, and the acquiree none, so the difficulty of altering an already understood and entrenched system is not present.

The new entity without a formal planning system of its own, however, will definitely experience culture shock. The first reaction is always resistance. "We're too busy operating a business to spend all the time required to do this kind of detailed planning." "Our situation changes fast. By the time we get all this stuff in writing, it will be outdated." "You're asking for a lot of sensitive stuff. If it's in print, it will somehow find its way into the hands of our competitors." And the oldest cliché of all: "Look, we understand our business, you don't. Just let us go on operating as we have been doing. Don't rock the boat."

How to proceed? To minimize conflict and save time for everyone, the introduction of the corporation's planning system should be done at the top. The corporate president, planning vice president, and the headquarters executive to whom the new acquisition is to report should meet with the head of the new subsidiary and his direct reports.

There should ensue a presentation by the headquarters people of the evolution of planning in the corporation, the methodology used and annual timetables, and why it is needed. This last is most important. The president should participate actively in the presentation, explaining past planning successes and *failures*, and discussing what is needed and expected of the planning process in the future.

The acquisition executives are given plenty of opportunity to express doubts and fears. All the standard objections should be given a hearing, examined carefully, and then the vital nature of the planning process to the future of the corporation and the new subsidiary is firmly reiterated.

This procedure won't automatically result in full acceptance and quiet all objections. It will, however, bring home to the key people how important the matter is to their new bosses and leave no doubt that the job must be well done, for their individual benefit as well as for the corporation.

If, instead, the corporate headquarters sends out a financial person and a planner, neither corporate vice presidents, who, plan book in hand, sit down with lower-level people at the subsidiary to explain what is desired, acceptance will come very slowly and painfully. Worse, the initial plans produced will be worthless.

Once over the initial hurdle of the top-level meeting, then the headquarters functional vice presidents—of marketing finance, manufacturing, engineering, and employee relations—needs to explain their functional parts of the planning process to their opposite numbers in the new entity. What kinds of exhibits and written commentary are used and why. How markets and share of available market are defined. What definitions of productivity, inventory turns, asset utilization, return on investment, are to be used. What guidelines are to be used for specifying cost reductions, and on what timing such planned reductions are to be reflected and forecast in profit and loss statements. How capital investment money commitments and expected timing for the cash outlays are to be presented, etc.

Just because such a myriad of details is involved in good business planning, getting the new entity off on the right foot is so important that it requires some headquarters presidential and vice-presidential time. If not done first at the top but delegated to lower levels, the initiation of planning the first time around will prove a tremendous irritant and time waster, at both headquarters and the new subsidiary. At the acquisition because of the "blind leading the blind" syndrome, as the people try to interpret the planning guide to each other. At headquarters because of the many and repeated questions coming from the subsidiary: "What is really wanted?" "How do we calculate plant efficiency?" "Does market definition include product lines we don't have yet?" and on and on.

So the acquiring corporation should do the introduction of the business planning right the first time, from the top down. It is corporate top executives' time well spent.

If the acquired company is large and already has in place a written plan and an ongoing planning process, then the detailed treatment of plans required by the larger corporation will not be such a wrenching shock. Still needed, however, is introduction of the acquirer's planning philosophy to the key people of the new subsidiary, and discussion of what changes may be needed in the acquiree's existing approach to planning.

For example, the acquiring company may be firmly committed to the early Boston Consulting Group philosophy: plan to gain share, increase volume, which reduces cost, so prices can be lowered to gain more share, etc. The new entity may be using the Strategic Planning Associates approach, which concentrates more on evaluation of alternative strategies in the context of what competitors may be expected to do. Or both the acquiring corporations and the new entity may have home-brewed planning methodologies that have evolved over the years and seem well suited to their businesses.

In any case, the top management "summit" meeting is still the best, least troublesome way to initiate understanding of what the new parent needs and expects from division business plans.

All of the differences in financial exhibits to be included, the definitions of market size and growth rates, the amount of detail to be used in discussing capital expense projections and engineering projects, etc., must be covered with the acquisition's top people. Importantly, it should be first introduced by only the president, planning vice president, and the HQ executive responsible for the new acquisition. Then afterward the lower-level people should be assigned to begin business planning methodology and timing discussions with their opposite numbers at the acquisition.

Beyond understanding methodology and the mechanics of plan presentation, the chief problems will come from the need for mutual appreciation of what role the acquired company is expected to fulfill in the overall corporate plan. To be sure, before the acquisition this was considered. The acquiring corporation was looking, say, for a position in a new field of promising growth and decided it was cheaper to buy an existing company than to try to build this new business internally. Or the acquired entity is in a closely related, even overlapping, product area, where the acquirer wants participation to broaden its existing business. There is usually some synergistic reason behind acquisitions (despite numerous exceptions) that both the parent and its new division understood during the acquisition negotiations.

But now the problems of allocation of resources within the larger corporation, the relative importance of the new entity in the total corporate structure, the degree to which the aspirations and plans of the acquired company mesh with corporate ideas and expectations, must be clarified and quantified in the business plan.

The new entity's most strongly held beliefs and assumptions about its markets, competitors, products, capabilities, will have to be put under a spotlight, challenged, questioned. Sacred cows will be kicked all over the place.

And also, of course, the new division will find it has a new kind of competition, internal competitors in the corporation. Competitors for available funds, for favorable consideration of important new projects, for general understanding at headquarters of the kind of business the new division is in, its opportunities and its problems.

Following the preparation of an initial business plan by the acquired entity comes its review by the corporate headquarters. This first exposure to the advances of an eager HQ staff can be a traumatic experience for the new people.

The most common mistake made by the corporate HQ in these first plan reviews is to try to point the bewildered new division in too many directions.

First and foremost is the urge to think big. The multi-billion dollar corporation headquarters people look at the acquisition doing 100 million dollars in sales and wonder what it would take to make it 200 million. The acquired company has been growing at, say, 10 percent per year, so plans an increase next year to 110 million dollars of sales.

"Why not plan to grow much faster?" asks the corporate VP of planning. "What keeps you from going to 120 million next year, and doubling your present size in three or four years?" "Well," answers the new division's head, "our market is growing at about a 10 percent rate." "OK, so gain share. All you need for an additional 10 million sales is another 2 percent of available. Surely with a little more sales effort, you can do that."

The division head looks at his marketing manager for support. That woman, quick on the uptake, realizes that her head is on the line if unrealistic sales increases are built into a plan. "This is a very competitive industry we're in," she states. "Our share, at 20 percent of the available, is quite high now. We could trigger a price war if we try to increase share any more, and in a hurry."

"So there's a price war, so what?" continues the corporate planning vice president. "I see you claim in your plan to have the lowest manufacturing costs in your industry. That being so, you'd chase the other guys off the field, unless they want to go broke."

"Wait a minute," protests the acquisition's financial officer, "we're supposed to make money, aren't we? How long would this price war go on, and how low will the prices go? We don't have that much margin to play with."

"Well, you have to tell me the answers to all those questions," remorselessly continues the headquarters VP. "Work up some price/volume/cost analyses, and redo the plan to include them. I specifically want to see how you would look at 120 million sales next year instead of 110.

While the division people are unhappily contemplating the pile of new work required to comply, and at the same time realizing that the questions so quickly tossed out are virtually unanswerable, the HQ manufacturing man takes up the cudgels. "If you double your present volume, won't your total manufacturing costs drop 25 or 30 percent? That would allow a helluva price decrease."

The new division's manufacturing head doesn't know where this discussion is leading, but is becoming aware that he probably won't like the destination. "I can't double production in our present space," he demurs, "a new factory would be needed. Anyway, the type of high-speed rotary equipment we use takes over a year to purchase and get installed. We couldn't handle a quick big increase in sales."

"I don't like to hear that kind of defeatist talk from a manufacturing man," says the staff expert. "How many shifts are you working?" "Three shifts, to best utilize our high-speed equipment, and six days a week." "Well, work Sundays too. That step alone will increase your output 16 percent!" "Thanks for the suggestion," mutters the division man.

No area will escape unscathed. Besides the price/volume suggestions, the marketing manager will be urged to consider various new products and new markets. She will be asked why international sales are so low. Has she really looked at the market in South America, especially Brazil? The controller will be told that the new division's accounts receivable days are far too high to meet with corporate approval. The 45 days must be reduced to 40 next year, fewer the year after. The engineering manager will be questioned closely on the use of microchips in designs. Why aren't more of them being used, and sooner?

Let's draw a curtain over the rest of this painful scene. It is repeated innumerable times in business plan review meetings all over the country. The discussion ranges far and wide and all too frequently ends up making hash out of the plan presented by the new division.

The headquarters staff is behaving normally. This brusque treatment of the submitted plan is what the existing divisions of the corporation go through every year. But they have the great benefit of experience. They can sort through the chaff quickly to find the wheat in the staff questions, objections, and suggestions. They also have a history of accomplishment, or lack of it, of which both they and the headquarters people are fully aware.

Market share, pricing, and the basic competitive picture have been reviewed and debated in previous meetings. The staff experts know where the division people stand on the issues of what is feasible and what is not in their business. The line people know where the staff believes they could and should be making gains. The division engineering manager has made his case before that he is progressively utilizing microchips step by step in the electronics of his new designs, as each generation of his long-lived equipment products becomes obsolete. The manufacturing manager does not try to operate seven days a week, because of both equipment maintenance needs and lack of available Sunday labor in the plant location, and the headquarters manufacturing staff knows it.

In every corporation there do exist some standard subjects of debate at planning meetings. The circular, because going nowhere, discussion of these select items is repeated over and over with no decision. There is no final resolution either because there is no good answer—some business problems have no solution—or because the contending parties both carry considerable weight in the organization.

Even as decisive and normally very impatient an individual as Harold Geneen recognized and tolerated some repeated circular discussions at ITT's business review meetings. During one such, Geneen suddenly interrupted the participants. "You missed your cue," he said to one vice president. "When he says 'The problem is a policy split of business by that customer,' you are supposed to say, 'No, it's a product quality problem.' Please stay awake."

A final, and very important, consideration in the way business plan review meetings are handled is the current financial performance of the division under scrutiny.

When things are going well, sales increasing, earnings in good shape, cash flow positive, return on investment above corporate targets, the meetings can be a pleasure. Nitpicking is nonexistent. Even valid criticism is muted. The important issues are discussed soberly, in quiet voices. The division people exude confidence. The staff personnel are relaxed and appreciative. Largeness of spirit is manifest in mutual compliments and expressions of hope for a golden future in which all will participate.

But when the review is of an underachieving division, all hell can break loose and frequently does. The headquarters staff arrives armed to the teeth with charts and reports illuminating in excruciating detail the manifold faults and failings of the division people. The line people are suitably humble, avoiding any suspicion of illusions of grandeur, making no bright remarks this time at the expense of staff.

The review itself usually strays from its purpose of planning for the future, and somehow concentrates on past, especially recent past, derelictions of duty on the part of the division. This focus does enable the corporate president and various vice presidents to blow off steam, which no doubt has a therapeutic effect for them but is hard for those on the receiving end.

A review of actual results versus business plan projections, however, is still in the future for the new acquisition. It has first to obtain approval of an initial plan. A wise corporate management will keep the gloves on the first time the acquisition presents a plan. It is simply not necessary to take it apart piece by piece and then ask the new division to reassemble it in several different ways. It is not productive to browbeat the new managers at planning time just to let them know who's boss.

At the same time it remains essential for a multi-division corporation to insist that planning methodology be good and that each division produce a plan that hangs together and is realistic. Headquarters needs to understand what the division is trying to accomplish, and how it expects to reach its targets. The acquisition needs to understand the broad corporate goals, and how the divisions are expected to contribute to realizing them.

A good business plan is the best vehicle for accomplishing this desirable two-way understanding, for establishing the new division's place in the corporate sun, for assuring a fair share of corporate resources and rewards. On its side, the corporate headquarters will be anxious to get a good and realistic understanding of the new entity. What is really there, and what can realistically be expected to be accomplished.

Therefore, developing a mutually satisfactory business plan is a matter of urgency for both the corporate headquarters and the acquisition and justifies top management participation from the beginning.

Further suggestions for minimizing the tears and travail of initial business planning for the newly acquired company are considerations of timing and content.

On timing, make the submission of a complete plan, on the corporation's usual schedule, effective the *second* year after acquisition. Use the first year for the get-acquainted, mutual understanding and acceptance process. If the new entity has an existing planning process, let it produce one more plan in the old format (they will all be in English and use normal numerals, so it can be understood), with transition to the new format to follow in the second year. It might even occur that some aspects of the acquisition's plans merit incorporation into the parent corporation's approach. If so, it's great morale booster for the new people, and softens considerably their worries about the corporate planning process.

On content, where formal business planning, that is, producing a book, is new to the acquired company and therefore represents quite a serious burden, why not let it produce a shorter, less detailed version of a regular division plan. This in the first and perhaps the second year, before going to the full bells and whistles treatment.

Finally, what is wrong with a graduated scale of complexities and detail in the divisional plans? The largest, most important operations be required to produce a very detailed and even voluminous plan, smaller divisions to have a truncated version, less detail, less nits and gnats. This puts less of a burden on the smaller divisions, which have fewer people to handle the planning work.

10
PUBLIC RELATIONS

WHAT IS CONSIDERED a good public relations program in any large corporation looks considerably different when viewed from headquarters or from a division. The headquarters people, especially the top executives, are primarily interested in favorably impressing the financial world: bankers, fund managers, market analysts, investors. A division is chiefly interested in wooing two constituencies: customers and the local communities in which it operates facilities.

Corporate headquarters wants a public relations program of press releases emphasizing good financial performance; meetings with security analysts and fund managers to promote the stock; discussions with bankers on how well the corporation is handling its debt to equity ratio and cash; advertisements featuring the corporation rather than any specific product line. Of course the corporation's spread of product interest gets mentioned, especially in the annual report, but from an olympian height, chiefly to demonstrate that the corporation has chosen good areas on which to concentrate, promising sales and earnings growth for the future.

The divisions, on the other hand, consider a good public relations program to be one that concentrates first on impressing customers with specific new and improved product introductions, through application literature and product advertising; making a good appearance at trade shows; announcing important local personnel changes; promoting factory tours by customers. Second, it concentrates on creating and maintaining a favorable climate of opinion in the communities in which it operates. The division wants to be seen as a helpful citizen, maintaining a good place to work, paying taxes, interested in the city or town's welfare, providing jobs. To this end the division's people are encouraged to participate in local activities.

The division employees will belong to every manner of civic and social organization, help in charitable fund raising drives, assist on planning commissions, and generally try to maintain a favorable climate of public opinion toward the company. The company will make donations to the United Way, to a building fund for the local hospital, to the new art museum. Open house days will be celebrated in a festive way, with one and all invited to visit the plant to see what goes on, partake of coffee and cake, and have a chance to shake the hand of the plant manager.

Because of these differing viewpoints of what constitutes a good public relations program, there will always be tension between headquarters and the divisions on how best to spend the money available. Headquarters may see great value in making a substantial contribution to some well-publicized national fund raising campaign, but little in making small contributions to the YMCAs in the 50 communities in which the corporation has facilities. Headquarters will want the division's PR person to spend more time with the local Merrill, Lynch manager and less with the superintendent of schools. The divisions would prefer that the corporate annual reports *not* be sent to their best customers, because it will brag about improvements in the corporate financial performance. This leads to many a salesperson being shown his own annual report by a purchasing agent, who then makes ribald comments on the product prices he's being asked to pay. Headquarters, of course, wants the annual report featured everywhere.

Against this background appears an acquired company. Having previously been independent, it will have made a tenuous, often uneasy, compromise of its own between the desires of its headquarters PR and those of its local facilities. Perhaps its president participates in many civic activities, even has encouraged employees to run for public office: school board, say, city council, or mayor. Perhaps the reverse is true. The president wants noses to the product and customer grindstone and lets local opinion take care of itself. In any event there will be an advertising program, press releases are being issued, favorite trade shows are being attended, and the image is being polished in various ways with customers.

As in other functional areas, corporate headquarters public relations will want to mold the new entity in its own image and as soon as possible. "Stop making press releases locally. We will issue any and all releases from headquarters." "Don't talk to any newspapers or trade magazines. Refer them to headquarters." "No local contributions are to be made to anything without corporate review and approval." "For God's sake get that manager off the mayor's financial committee. We don't want to be seen as involved in politics."

The adjustment for the new division can be rough, especially if its previous practice has been quite different from the new parent's approach. The basic golden rule of "Go slow" emphatically applies here.

Don't change the existing pattern of local contributions to worthy causes in the first year. Time enough for that when next year's planning and budgeting is being done. In the meantime the acquired entity is introduced to the new parent's approach to contributions; discussions between the parent public relations people and the local ones take place; and mutual understanding is developed.

Some of the status quo will have to be changed, but certainly not all. Local particular situations can be accommodated. The president of the acquired entity sits on the board of trustees of the local university, so, not surprisingly, his largest corporate annual donation of funds goes to that institution. For reasons of local prestige, continuity, not wanting to appear a Scrooge, the new parent permits this situation to continue, even if corporate policy points contributions in other directions.

Relations with the local newspapers, and to a lesser extent, the trade press, is always a tricky area of intermittent irritation between an acquisition and its new parent. Most corporate headquarters public relations people, backed up by the president, want to keep firmly in their hands any contacts with the general newspapers. The desire, of course, is twofold: to try to obtain favorable mention when the corporate name appears in the press; and to ensure that a subsidiary's people don't make statements at variance with the existing corporate party lines.

Alas, the attempt to so control press mention is doomed to failure, even though the attempt is always made, with varying degrees of effort.

The common policy approach of most corporations is to instruct local people to refer all inquiries from general newspapers to headquarters, and to communicate with reporters and editors only via official press releases. This is unworkable, of course. Some unpleasant event occurs, say a sizable layoff of people at the subsidiary's factory. The local newspaper calls up and wants comments. The inquiring reporter is referred to the official press release, and also to corporate headquarters, but he won't be put off. He has questions. "Are there plans for still further layoffs?" "Is this a first step toward closing the plant completely?" "Is it true that you are trying to eliminate the union at the factory by firing militant people?"

It is useless for the local subsidiary's manager or public relations person to say "We have no comment beyond the press release." If the local newspaper wants a story, it will get one or invent one. A reporter starts calling other people in the company, contacts employees who have just been laid off, or friends of employees, and soon he has plenty of material, especially from disgruntled employees, present or past, who are characterized as "sources within the company," or "close to the company." Not surprisingly, the story that eventually emerges can be extremely fanciful, bearing an almost unrecognizable relationship to the real situation.

Given these facts of life, the corporate headquarters should not try to enforce a policy whereby only headquarters people talk to the press. The local manager, along with his key people, is the best chance the corporation has of presenting its activities in a favorable light and interpreting unhappy local news in a larger context.

The current layoff situation may be real, but there are always activities offering the hope of a good future: new products coming along, capital investments being made, additional markets appearing. The headquarters PR people simply do not know many of these aspects as well as the local managers do. Therefore, let the local people represent the corporation to the local press.

The point is even clearer when considering a company large enough in its community for its president or general manager to rub elbows with editors of the local newspapers. How can this top local representative of the corporation plead the fifth amendment to her luncheon or golf companions? She can't, so she talks to them, with or without coporate policy approval.

Relations with the trade press are easier because of their considerable knowledge of the industry in which the company participates. The trade press sees developments in the context of existing customers' demand and of competitive activities. The trade press people have a better understanding of the evolution of the industry, the stature of the company's products, and its position with customers. Unfavorable happenings are less likely to be seen and presented as forerunners of total disaster.

At the same time, trade press relations are also subject to strain, just because of the always inherent possibly adversary relationship between any newspaper and the object of its attention.

A basic problem does exist in corporate relationships with the public press for which there is simply no good answer. It is that the pace of almost all businesses is much too slow for competent treatment by newspapers and other "now" media. A newspaper is oriented to now: what happened yesterday, is happening today, and may occur tomorrow. It presents what is going on dramatically and in a shout. The media believe they must present everything as something new, just discovered—news!

A business, however, simply does not—cannot—make exciting things happen from one day to the next. A business program was initiated perhaps five years ago. It is painstakingly worked along to fruition, with many detours and disappointments along the way, until it culminates in a product or a useful service. If a newspaper then does a story on the project, it will do so with a headline like, "Local Company Discovers Winner," or, "New Invention Promises Revolution" in something or other. The impression given is that someone had a good idea last week, and, presto, there is a completely new thing in existence this morning. This does not foster realistic understanding of how business works.

Unfortunately for business also, the media love to work along the "worst case" trail. Bad news, editors assure us, is what people want to read about. Thus any disappointing happening at a local company, such as orders slowing down, some people laid off, or a new product not fulfilling expectations, is grist for the disaster mill. "So orders have fallen off," says the reporter, "What if they continue to drop?" "Well," replies the plant manager, "if they just keep going down, I suppose we would eventually have to let some people go." The headline the next day will read, "Local Plant Layoffs Seen."

The totally different time scales along which the media and businesses operate ensures continuing irritation with each other, entirely apart from the all too real ideological differences and misunderstandings.

Moving from the general area of public relations to a particular aspect of it, consider advertising. There is almost always a struggle between corporate headquarters and the division's advertising people. The HQ staff sees the basic purpose of advertising as the enhancement of the corporate image. They want total corporate name polishing: our company is strong, successful, on the move. Our products do lots of good things for lots of people. The divisions, on the other hand, want advertising to promote very specific products and services: what our product can do for specific customers, what features make it so useful, what new applications it can handle.

This difference in viewpoint is readily understood by realizing that headquarters people, particularly the top executives, are simply interested in impressing a different constituency. Headquarters wants the favorable attention of potential or actual shareholders, of the financial community, of stock market analysts, of fund managers.

The top executives are interested in advertising and promotional material that paints with a broad brush. We are "an energy company," "an electronics company," "a high technology company," is the preferred kind of theme. The larger the corporation, of course, the more necessary is this kind of oversimplification. Really explaining all the corporation's product lines in broad-brush advertisements is not possible.

The divisions, though, want very specific product advertising aimed at the customers in their marketplace. A division manufacturing parts for commercial aircraft wants ads that will score with Boeing, Lockheed, and McDonnell Douglas people. A sister division making television sets want advertising aimed at the household consumer.

Now since this diversity of advertising purpose is so readily understandable, why is there continuing tension and friction on the matter between HQ staff advertising people and their colleagues at the divisions? There are two principal reasons. One is a persuasive belief at most corporate headquarters that the individual product divisions are aided in their sales efforts by general corporate image-enhancement advertising. The second is that HQ marketing people find it all but impossible to keep their noses out of the division's product advertising programs.

The dogma at corporate headquarters that general image adverstising helps the divisions sell their products runs deep. That this cherished belief is simply not so is clearly shown by considering specifics. In the case of an industrial product, that is, one specified by engineers and bought by professional purchasing agents, it is the quality and performance specifications, along with price and past performance, that determine whether a sale is made or not. The ability of the omnipresent competition also makes a big difference. What make *no* difference is that division's corporate parent advertising, "We are a leading high-technology company."

No, in industrial products, the divisions of a large corporation have to stand on their own feet. The fact that one Westinghouse division makes excellent turbines does not aid its sister division in selling switch-gear.

In consumer products, the same situation exists. In these product areas, the potential buyers do not write the product specifications and do not have professional buyers working for them. Still, our product choices do not depend on general corporate advertising. For example, General Electric spends a lot of money on total corporate image polishing, especially on television, which reaches consumers directly. Yet the share of available market that GE's consumer products divisions obtain varies widely. General Electric has a large share of all refrigerators sold in the Untied States, but a very small share of TV sets, even though both are pushed via general corporate advertising.

It is difficult for corporate headquarters people to accept, but the fact is that though broad-brush corporate image enhancement may impress Wall Street and the banks, it does not help its subsidiaries sell product.

The problem of staff marketing people wanting to get involved in division advertising programs is a difficult one to overcome. In its most common form, the HQ approach seems reasonable on the surface.

"We want to utilize a common logo and a common visual appearance of the ads, for example, the amount of space devoted to text as against pictures or drawings, the typeface to be used, placement and size of the headline, etc." Why do we want this? "So customers and the financial community will recognize the family appearance of our ads, thus giving added impact."

Well, common logo, OK, of course. But all ads to *look* the same? How is this to be accomplished? "We'll make up a book of instructions, with illustrations, which your advertising departments will all utilize. No problem."

Then the instructions arrive, with ambiguities, many special cases not covered, a lot of things requiring clarification. Now the conscientious division advertising people have to enter into numerous and detailed discussions with the HQ staff people. The result? You have the HQ marketing people spending a lot of time virtually having to run the advertising programs of all the divisions. They might enjoy this, but they shouldn't be allowed to do it. It's wasteful duplication of effort, and also, as with so many staff/line problem areas, it saps the initiative of the division people. They become increasingly dependent on directions from HQ, whose people, being remote from the particulars of the division battlefield, are going to make unnecessary mistakes.

The best approach to successfully integrating the public relations work of a new acquisition is the clear delineation of what work is to be done at the local operations, and what work is to be done only by headquarters. With this checklist, and the careful discussion of each item, the appropriate level of local public relations activity will emerge. This level will be considerable, thus quieting the fears of the acquired public relations people that their function may be entirely eliminated. The clarification of spheres of activity will also give the acquired people a good understanding of the parent corporation's modus operandi in the public relations field, enhancing local understanding and support of corporate public relations objectives.

Acquisitions are made because the acquirer believes the new entity will enhance the existing corporate structure: extending its range into related product fields; getting into desirable new fields immediately through an existing company; or even just adding assets and sales volume at what seems a good price. Whatever the reason, the acquirer then wants his corporation to gain in prestige and visibility through recognition that the previously independent Alpha Company is now part of the Omega Corporation. The acquirer wants to gain with all its corporate constituencies: customers, investors, employees, suppliers, even the general public in places where it has facilities. Also, of course, there is satisfaction in the feeling that this is one in the eye for competition and should be known.

Now, how does the acquirer approach gaining the desired recognition of linkage between the parent corporation and its new entity? There will be a news release from corporate headquarters that will be mentioned by the *Wall Street Journal*, of course. Also, the trade press and the local newspapers where corporate headquarters and the new entity are located will print part of the news release. The corporation will proudly mention its new division in the next annual report, and that's about it.

Does that get the job done? Hardly. Important investors—funds, banks, brokerage houses—all read the *Wall Street Journal*. But millions of actual or potential customers—the most important constituency—don't, nor will they get the word on the six o'clock TV news. All those customer engineers, manufacturing people, purchasing agents and general managers, who make or break a company, will not at first take any notice of the new linkup. Further, they simply don't care. The fact of the acquisition is a nothing to them.

And that's as it should be. The acquired company's products are being purchased simply because their particular combination of product quality, price, service, and general record is preferred over that of its competitors. If customers happen to know about or hear of the acquisition, it won't make one iota of difference in their world. They're buying because they like the present and usual performance of the acquired entity. They would like it to get even better in the future. They mildly hope it won't get worse.

Simple example: Because it was such a gigantic acquisition—actually made the six o'clock TV news—many more people than is usual know that du Pont has acquired Conoco. Well, how many people who admired du Pont now stop their car at a Conoco station instead of their regular Texaco, Mobil, or Exxon? And the other way around—how many Conoco customers are switching to du Pont products just because of the acquisition?

However, in spite of these rather basic considerations, there exists in most acquirers a strong belief that it is important to force recognition of the new linkup upon all constituencies, and that such recognition will benefit both the acquired Alpha Company and the parent Omega Corporation.

How is this gone about? The most frequently tried method is the one that causes the most trouble in the acquired company both practically and emotionally. An approach that is guaranteed to bruise egos and raise hackles, produce guerrilla warfare, and generate rancor and demoralization among the troops. I mean—change the name. The idea is that the Alpha Company name will cease to exist. The new entity will become the widget division of the Omega Corporation. Brilliantly simple in theory; makes no sense in practice.

What do you think is the reaction in the acquired company? Anger and dismay, of course. Over a long period of years—20, 40, 60—Alpha Company has labored to make its name a byword in the industry; there exist hard-won recognition in the trade of its brand name and respect for its past accomplishments and current performance. The employees have pride in their name as a symbol of achievement and excellence. To toss all this lightly aside is almost always a serious mistake, but it is obviously a very tempting one to many corporate strategies since it is tried so often.

"A rose by any other name would smell as sweet." True, but how do you get from here to there. If roses were called sesors, how many people would go out to smell the sesors in bloom? Eventually, of course, the excellence of the sesors' scent would begin to attract a larger and larger following, but how long would it take? In the meantime, what a waste from the name change.

As I have said, the "eliminate the old name" is *tried* often, because now the practical difficulties operate to slow down and very often eventually derail any name change program.

When ITT began to make its numerous acquisitions in the 1960s, President Geneen wanted the ITT name to supersede the existing company names. He was looking for investor recognition that ITT was a large, diversified corporation on the move. He also shared the mistaken belief of many that the smaller acquired companies would benefit with *customers* from use of the larger corporation's name.

So directions were issued: Cannon Electric was to become ITT Connectors; General Controls was to become ITT Controls; Surprenant was to become ITT Wire and Cable; Bell and Gossett was to become ITT Pumps, and on and on. Headquarters' staff pushed, prodded, and threatened the newly acquired companies.

The acquired companies naturally resisted. They presented numerous arguments, emotional as well as practical. The whole desired fabric of togetherness and mutual support with the acquisitions became grievously unraveled. "You mean our catalogs, our advertising and promotional material, stationery, invoices, signs on our buildings, on our trucks, all this is to be changed? How long will that take? And is headquarters going to pay for all these changes?" "That customer engineer who is used to reaching for the Cannon Electric catalog when designing—how long will it take to educate him that the same product is now in a different colored catalog called ITT Connectors? Why open that window of opportunity for our competitors?" "Our salespeople work for Cannon and are proud of it. ITT is a remote thing to them. Why complicate their allegiances?"

And the acquired companies also counterattacked. "ITT has a poor reputation among our customers. It isn't smart even to emphasize that we are now part of ITT." "Our salespeople will willy-nilly have to get involved in customer problems of other ITT divisions. It will reduce their effectiveness in selling our stuff." "Our name is better known in our industry than ITT. Why not change the ITT name?"

And all this commotion didn't help at all in the basics, that is, the subsidiary's efforts to sell, to manufacture, to produce good financial results. Rather it wasted executives' time, alarmed and irritated the employees unnecessarily and, obviously, exacerbated headquarters/division relations.

Well, what happened? As many of you know from his reputation, and others from direct experience, Harold Geneen is a very determined executive, and he wanted the name changes made. So the battle raged for a long time. Finally, however, Geneen saw that the cost—not in dollars, but in poisoned relationships within the corporation—was too high. Being a brillant and basically fair man, he also acknowledged that there was merit in the arguments put forth by the acquired companies. Still convinced, however, that for the long haul he wanted the ITT name on all those acquisitions—he's also a very stubborn man—a two-step approach was launched.

The first step was to be a linkage of names for some indefinite period, and the second was then ultimately to drop the various company names, using only ITT. Thus Cannon Electric became ITT Cannon, Bell and Gossett became ITT Bell and Gossett, etc. This was about 15 years ago, and the second step of dropping the old company names has never been taken, nor do I believe it ever will be.

A similar situation occurred in General Instrument some five years ago. General Instrument was originally a capacitor and rectifier company founded in the late 1930s. It grew, but slowly, until the late 1960s when the then president, Monte Shapiro, launched a brillantly successful acquisition program. By 1970, General Instrument had acquired industry leaders in several fields: Jerrold, the largest manufacturer of cable television equipment in the United States; American Totalisator, which manufactures the computer-controlled tote board used at 80 percent of U.S. race tracks, as well as computerized off-track betting and state lottery equipment; C. P. Clare, the largest manufacturer of sealed reed relays for the telecommunications equipment field; and several others.

The question of subsidiaries' name changes to reinforce the overall corporate image came up from time to time, but nothing concrete was announced until the mid-1970s. Then one year, at a meeting of chief headquarters people and the general managers of all the subsidiaries, a remarkable presentation was made by the marketing vice president and the public relations director. The marketing VP led off by declaring, "From tonight on, there is to be no more Jerrold, no more American

Totalisator, no more C. P. Clare, etc. From tonight on, we are all General Instrument: General Instrument Cable Television, General Instrument Relays, and so forth." But the rationale then presented for dropping the subsidiary names was pure Catch-22.

The public relations director took the rostrum and stated that we would readily understand the need for the change in names when we saw the results of a survey he had just completed. He then displayed a chart that had a General Instrument" printed in large letters at the top, and the subsidiaries' names grouped together on the rest of the chart. "Our study shows," he said, "that this name," pointing to General Instrument, "Is not as well known in many places as these names," pointing to Jerrold, American Totalisator, Clare, etc. "Now," he said, "we are going to fix this situation by eliminating all these other names and using only General Instrument." And people say there's no humor in business!

In General Instrument's case, fortunately, the pragmatic good sense of Chairman and President Frank Hickey prevented real damage from being done. The program died shortly, except that the names of a few of the smallest subsidiaries were changed. Instead of eliminating the important and well-known trade names, they were subsequently linked to General Instrument as in the ITT case.

More recently, Hickey has had second thoughts about even the few names that were changed and is considering going back to the old ones. One such was Chicago Miniature Lamp, whose name was changed to General Instrument Lamp. Today, several years after the change, a poll of customers, distributors, and representatives has shown overwhelming preference for the old name—which had been used, known, and respected in the trade for forty years.

The impulse, or temptation, to change names continues, however, despite all the precedent and logic that says, "Don't do it." In March 1982, United Technologies put large ads in the various business publications announcing that its subsidiary, American Bosch, would henceforward have a new trade name, United Technologies.

The rationale given in the ads illustrates clearly the confusion that exists in many corporate headquarters when thinking about the value of names. It emphasized the point that United Technologies was chosen as the new trade name for American Bosch in order to make clear UT's corporate commitment to worldwide automotive industry.

Make what clear to whom? American Bosch has been a well-known and highly respected name in the automotive industry for over 35 years.

The automotive engineers who specify fuel injection systems and ignition systems, the purchasing agents who place orders for them, and the executives in the industry, all know American Bosch as a reliable, high-quality supplier. Changing the well-known name to United Technologies does nothing for the customers of American Bosch, except perhaps irritate them. You can be sure the key people in this situation—the customers—perceive no sudden new "commitment" in the name change. American Bosch *is* committed to the automotive industry. It is Bosch's reason for being, and many customers will continue to refer to American Bosch as Bosch, long after the headquarters people who perpetrated the name change have disappeared from the scene.

The fact is that this kind of name change is not really aimed at customers. It is aimed at investors. The corporation hopes to make investors—Wall Street in general—more aware of the corporate name by plastering it on well-known subsidiaries. But it doesn't help because investment managers in banks, brokerage houses, pension funds, insurance companies, don't read product catalogs, nor do they buy diesel ignition systems. They will continue to be aware of United Technologies as UTX, a well-managed conglomerate with a good track record. Putting the name United Technologies on products until now bearing the trade name American Bosch won't sell a single share of UTX stock to the investment managers. Nor will it sell a single ignition system to an engineer or purchasing agent who wouldn't have bought it as American Bosch.

These examples should be proof enough of the correctness of the basic point. Well-known company and trade names should be left alone after an acquisition. Not only are they very valuable in themselves, but the problems associated with pushing a name change through an acquisition are simply not worth the effort required and the pernicious furor it arouses.

11
CONSULTANTS

THE SERVICES UTILIZED from outside a corporation's own walls include banking, legal and patent, personnel benefits administration (now required by law), search, and, in the extreme, consulting services.

Why are outside consultants used at all by large multi-division corporations? After all, isn't that what the HQ staff is intended to do? If the staff people in finance, manufacturing, marketing, etc., are really the experts they are supposed to be, who needs the fellows from outside the corporation altogether?

The answers are multitudinous. Firstly, there is the axiom that the bigger the corporate problem, the more likely it will be that outside consultants are invited in. Most presidents, with a good feel for survival tactics, realize telling their board that Booz, Allen, Hamilton or Boston Consulting Group is now digging into a major problem area, carries a lot more weight than saying that Smith and Jones from our own corporate staff are looking into the matter. Booz, Allen's answers may be no better than those provided by Smith and Jones, but the large consulting company's signature on a report has a lot of influence with U. S. corporations' boards of directors.

Secondly, there is the fact that all too frequently the HQ staff people are *not* broad-gauged enough in their functional area to be able to contribute more to solving a problem than the directly involved line people. The pious hope then is that a consulting firm may have the expertise needed somewhere among their people, so that the problem can be solved quickly.

Thirdly, and importantly, is the president introducing ourside consultants when he is contemplating some action that is sure to arouse ire and controversy among key personnel in the corporation. This tactic is most often utilized for high-level organizational changes, though also frequently for evaluation of major product efforts, acquisitions, or divestitures.

The president seldom is really at a loss with respect to which way to go, that is, which way he wants to go. However, he knows from bitter experience that the repercussions of disgruntlement among those against, or disappointment with, his preferred course of action can do a lot of damage internally. Previously good working relationships among senior executives can sour, harming not only morale but also operations. Already important, or promising, personnel might leave. So he sugarcoats the pill as best he can by obtaining the opinion he wants from respected consultants and then proceeds, asking all concerned to defer to the consultants' recommendations. "And if you still think they are cockeyed, don't argue with me, raise hell with the consultants."

None of the above should be interpreted to mean consultants are not really worth their fee. They can be very useful, if only as a sounding board for top management and in keeping all executive levels up-to-date on trends and innovations in their industry and functional areas of responsibility. Corporations do tend to become insular, loath to accept outside ideas that may be superior to whatever they are now doing, and so need a dose of outside pepper from time to time. Better a warning administered by a friendly consultant than an unexpected kick in the rear from a definitely unfriendly competitor.

Enter now consideration of the plight of a new acquisition, faced for the first time with outside consultants sent in by corporate headquarters. Initial contacts by corporate functional people have pinpointed various areas in the new division that need improvement, always the sooner the better.

In this case it is the production control system. The acquisition, respected in its field, has been in business 25 years, growing and prospering under the direct leadership of the founding entrepreneur. Last revised 10 years ago, the production control system was quite adequate for its day: production scheduling was done manually for a list of 200 product catalog numbers. Purchasing bought 4,000 different piece-parts, most of them in large quantities, sufficient for four or five months' production. Safety stocks in the storeroom and cached here and there on the factory floor kept production moving smoothly. Promised shipment times to customers averaged eight weeks, and were met 98 percent of the time.

But today the system has become woefully inadequate. Because of continuing new product introductions, customizing for large customers, and no product pruning, the number of product catalog numbers has quadrupled to 800. There are now 12,000 piece-parts for purchasing to order and store. Competitive pressure has reduced promised shipment times to four weeks. Scheduling the factory has become a nightmare for production control people and factory floor managers alike: inventory is climbing, on-time shipments percentages dropping, and of course the new acquisition is not meeting corporate targets for inventory turns or factory productivity.

In most cases the founding entrepreneur is gone, usually voluntarily, rather than face a future of numerous corporate HQ people looking over his shoulder, second-guessing, nitpicking. So awaiting the consultants with a mixture of hope and apprehension is a new general manager, either one of the former functional vice presidents, or a completely new man.

In either case, today the GM is frequently startled by the consultant's appearance. In his mind's eye the manager had seen a rather distinguished looking man with a good deal of silver hair among the black. But no, he is confronted with a briskly cheerful apple-cheeked youngster, who looks as though she might be just leaving college. And that, in fact, is the case. "Graduate of Harvard Business School," says the consultant. "Experience? Well, I learn fast." The manager gulps.

"I understand the problem here is material control. I'm sure it will present no great difficulty. We discussed several cases in point at Harvard," continues the consultant, "Lead me to the problem."

To cut the story short, the young woman observes, asks questions, studies reams of data, and finally returns to the GM with her recommendations. "First," she says, "obviously the whole process must be computerized: from entry of new orders, through calculating piece-part requirements, to production scheduling, computer-produced orders to piece-part vendors, and billing to customers as soon as the shipments are made. Second, inventory turnover is to be improved by reducing safety stocks; production is to be scheduled daily—by the computer—

rather than weekly, as now; vendors are to be allowed only two weeks to deliver their piece-parts. rather than the previous four weeks. Proceed to implement these recommendations ASAP, and your inventory control problem disappears," says the consultant confidently, and she leaves.

Well, what is the matter with the young woman's recommendations? Nothing. Nothing at all. Almost all of them are eminently sensible things to do. The problem is and was *implementation*. None of the consultant's ideas was a revelation to the line people at the division. All of them—and many others—had been and were being discussed. Efforts at implementation were being made.

All bill-of-material lists were being revised from the alpha-numeric numbering system originally applied by engineering to a new "universal" system suitable for computers (more numerics, less alphas, please). Computer terminals for order entry have just arrived and are being test-run. The short shipment times now required by competitive pressure mean that piece-parts will have to be ordered from vendors *before* specific customer orders are in hand for the division's products. Production control wants therefore a firm forecast from sales, by catalog number if you please, as to what orders will actually arrive each week. Sales argues in return that such accuracy is not possible.

The problem is not *what* to do, but implementing getting there. So why was the consultant brought in at all? She was *sent* in, remember, by corporate HQ. Net result, considerable time spent by the division's people educating the consultant, so she could then recommend to them that they should do what they are trying to do. This is useful?

The solution for a new acquisition is to keep outside consultants away from it for a healthy length of time, say two years. The new division will be getting all the attention it can handle from corporate HQ staff, all eager to learn the new business, to be able to talk about it knowledgeably at HQ, and even to contribute to its welfare, if possible.

Some readers may wonder what has happened to the earlier breed of consultants who would, if needed, move into an operation and do the implementation themselves, whether it took six months or a year. They are all but gone from the industrial scene, for two reasons, one good, and one unfortunate.

The good reason is the strong internal resistance encountered by an outside consultant actually moving into an operation and directly taking charge of necessary changes. He is regarded with the same affection as an occupying army would be by a fiercely nationalistic population. This resistance goes far toward negating the good hoped for from the consultant's expertise. His work is hampered and nitpicked at every step, and implementation moves very slowly, even gets sabotaged at various points along the way. Almost always better is for the consultant to study the situation, make recommendations, and depart, leaving the local people to do the job. This internal resistance can be deplored, but it is a fact of life.

The unfortunate reason why consultants seldom any more move into an operation to implement their suggested changes is that most of them today do not have the know-how required to translate recommendations into a finished new system. They know a good deal about forests, but individual trees they know not. Never having spent time—I mean months and years, not weeks—in lower-level operating positions, they simply do not have good standards in their heads with respect to the time required and the specific step-by-step actions needed to be taken by all functions in a business, in order to accomplish a broad recommendation, for example, "Put a lot more stuff on computers and things will move faster."

Every now and then the value of such basic line experience is rediscovered. A business periodical, with a straight face, publishes an article asserting that experienced people in a particular business are less likely to make serious mistakes in judgment than newcomers. A company president is actually quoted in a newspaper saying, "We forgot for a while that experience does count, but we are again aware of it." What is going on here? How old are these people making such a marvelous discovery?

No matter. The fact that lack of experience in a particular business does make a difference is an important reason why the young consultants just out of business school have had their halos knocked askew. People in business should be around a job long enough to have to recognize, live with, and correct their mistakes. Otherwise they become dilettantes, only dabbling with the problems of a business. Their understanding of what is going on and analysis of what might be better ways of doing things will be, and will remain, superficial.

And yet, working-level expertise simply cannot be expected from a young consultant. After all, the person who has spent months and years in operating positions ipso facto can't be the 25-year-old just graduated from Stanford Business School. And there is another very real factor operating here—the people who have the high degee of active intelligence, a sufficiently broad-guage view of the business world, and

and enough charisma to be good consultants to experienced high-level executives can't and won't spend a lot of time in pedestrian lower-level operating positions. It would drive them crazy and indeed be a wasteful use of valuable human resources.

A large corporation management area today where consultants are increasingly used is that of strategic business planning. This is congenial for both the consulting firms and their top management clients.

Most large consulting firms have seen their staffs become more and more concentrated at the top and bottom of the age scale. Their silver-haired partners grew up with the consulting business, which really began to proliferate only after World War II. Their increasingly numerous young people are only a few years out of business school, often with little or no work experience in the businesses for which they will be consulting. The senior people are well beyond dealing with the problems of manufacturing or engineering. They talk to the top management of corporations, and today they talk about strategy, not operations.

This is easier, of course. Imagination can take flight in many directions, unhampered by mundane worries about how to implement the strategies discussed. For the corporations' key executives, it is also a pleasant respite from the day-to-day struggle. Much better the consultant coming in to review strategic options, and hopefully to suggest some promising new ones, than to be there to probe into the shortcoming of a particular vice president's divisions.

One of the earliest and most successful of the emphases on strategic planning consultants has been the Boston Consulting Group. Their basic contribution was in two areas. First was popularizing the very useful "corporate portfolio" approach to evaluating a corporation's divisions. Second was the almost dogmatic insistence on the overwhelming importance of market share. Gain market share, which reduces costs through higher volume, which enables lowering prices, which will gain more market share, etc., until you are the dominant player in the field—so ran the dictum.

Of course if there are ten competitors in the field, and all of them embrace the "gain dominant market share" approach, the effect will be disastrous. Prices will drop through the floor, some companies will be forced to the wall, and the remaining ones will see profitability dwindle to the vanishing point. The only happy people around will be customers enjoying the price wars—for awhile. Then as the number of suppliers drops, and those that remain cut a lot of corners to reduce costs, the customers also suffer.

Since Boston Consulting's pioneering work, many consultants and corporate managements have adopted the "corporate portfolio" evaluation of divisional current situations and prospects. Most of them, however, have softened the "gain market share or else" dogma, including Boston Consulting itself in recent years.

A good consulting approach to strategic planning is that of making your plans in the context of what competitors may be expected to do. This view recognizes that the existence of real competitors puts restraints on blue-sky planning ideas. For example, you can be sure that your competitors *will* react to your reducing prices by lowering their own. Less brutal ways to gain share are needed: improvements to existing products, useful new product ideas, better coverage of promising sales prospects, shorter shipment times.

Many times a corporation's business planning manual is actually produced by its consultants, and they can be good ones. Better, however, is a business planning guide written within the corporation. This document, properly done, is more useful than a general one produced by a consultant. The home-made planning guide can more realistically reflect the particular crochets and foibles of a corporation: its history, the best way to portray knowledge of customers and competitors, the evolution of products technology, and expectations of future changes. The finest in-house planning guide I have ever encountered was that produced for General Instrument in 1977 by its then vice president for planning, Lorne Weil.

Besides business planning, the most active area for consultants today is that of the executive search—head hunting. This is a tender subject for corporate personnel departments. After all, recruiting has always been considered the preserve of the personnel people. Is the vice president for human resources not competent to seek out promising candidates for important positions in the corporation? And what about line management? If the corporation has a division active in the computer field, won't its management have a good idea of who's who and what's what among the good people in its competitors' employ?

Obviously, if the corporate board of directors has decided they need a new president to replace an incumbent, it will not ask the in-house personnel vice president to make the search. An outside search firm will be used to minimize premature disclosure of such a dramatic impending change. There are many executive recruiting situations, however, that could be handled quite adequately by in-house human resources/ personnel people but today are almost routinely sent out to search firms. The executive recruiting consultant is here in force.

The appearance of one on the scene anywhere, whether at corporate HQ or at a division, needless to say, causes anxiety. Who is going to be replaced? This understandable worry is greatly increased if the search firm's consultant puts in an appearance at a new acquisition. Rumors will fly.

Only a few of the top division people know that the consultant is there seeking new business. "We've done a lot of good work for the corporation you are now a part of," he says, "and we look forward to being able to help you meet your executive search needs in the future." "Thanks," says the division general manager, "we'll keep you in mind. Goodbye." But morale damage is done, because many people in the division will be waiting for a shoe or two to drop.

The answer? Just as in the case of other consultants, keep the executive search people out of the new division for a year or two.

Many outside services that the acquired entity is using will most probably be by local people or organizations that have been associated with its business for a long time. This includes a local legal firm, for both general and patent matters, a bank or two, insurance companies, and an outside auditing firm.

Now comes corporate headquarters, after the acquisition is completed, and all too often severs these well-established local relationships in a hurry. The headquarters staff people involved will ride roughshod over the acquired company's objections, usually in the name of lining up with corporate policy, or ensuring uniformity across the corporation. They will proceed as if quick change in these areas is a Very Important Matter.

The result is embarrassment and resentment on the part of the acquisition's personnel, who may well have worked with the affected outside people for a long time. They know them socially, may be neighbors, rub elbows at local affairs, serve together on civic committees. Of course there also occurs a strong and lasting loss of goodwill for the parent corporation on the part of the local people so brusquely pushed out of the picture. This can be accompanied by real financial hardship, at least until adjustments can be made, for a small legal or auditing firm.

Why do it so abruptly? There is no good reason. The golden rule is to make any necessary changes in the roster of outside services used by the acquisition over an extended period of time. Two or three years is needed and can readily be accommodated by the parent corporation with no noticeable adverse effect on financial results or reputation. Rather the opposite. The corporation will gain additional goodwill from both the acquired entity's people and the outside businesses affected. The parent will be regarded as fair and careful in its relationships with both its own people and others. A useful reputation for any corporation to have, and one that no amount of advertising will create, since actions, as always, speak louder than words.

When General Instrument acquired C. P. Clare of Chicago, in 1968, Clare had been using a small local legal firm ever since it was founded in 1937, a thirty-one year relationship. The legal services provided had been and were satisfactory in every respect. However, GI's general counsel had a policy of using the largest law firms available, on the reasonable theory that the range of talent and experience available in a large law firm should be greater than in a small one.

Clare's legal firm numbered a dozen or so lawyers at the time. The headquarters general counsel wanted to switch to one of the three largest Chicago law firms, one that fielded some 150 lawyers. In numbers there was no contest. However, the small firm's services to Clare over the years had been of impeccable quality. Was a change really necessary?

Well, general counsels in most corporations call the legal representation decisions, as they should. So we made the change. But the transition took place over a period of five years, during which the amount of legal work needed was shifted gradually to the large firm as new cases occurred. Also, and importantly, before the program to change the representation was formally decided, General Instrument's general counsel discussed his policy directly with the managing partner of Clare's old law firm. Of course the long-time Clare legal counsel would have preferred no change at all, but the period of time over which the transition took place minimized its disruptive effect, and reducing adverse effects after an acquisition is what wise managements will strive for in the integration process.

What to do about the outside auditors the acquired company has been using? They may be a small local firm, or perhaps one of the big seven. In either case, their services have been satisfactory, which is why they are handling the business.

In the case where the acquiree is using one of the major national accounting firms, the change can be made immediately with no real adverse effect. If the parent corporation uses Peat, Marwick, and the acquired entity uses Deloitre, Haskins and Sells, or vice versa, make the shift right away. The major national firms not only understand this, they wish it. None of them wants to be in the position of having to OK or cross-check the work of one of its competitors.

If the prevously independent company has been using a small local auditing firm, however, then go slow. The national firm handling the corporate account will push for picking up the new division's audit work, of course. It means additional business for them. But though they will cite the desirability of uniform audit practice across the corporation, and administrative efficiency resulting from one firm auditing the entire corporation, the change does not have to be made, and certainly not in a hurry. The unusual exception would be if the acquired entity is so large in the parent corporate picture that the transaction approaches a merger rather than an acquisition.

Therefore, as in the case of legal services, continue use of the local auditing firm for a year or two or three, so as to give them reasonable time to prepare for the loss of that business. This makes accepting the eventual change much easier for them and for your new local people.

12

USE OF
CORPORATE STAFF

THE NECESSARY INTERFACING between corporate-level staff of the parent and people of the new acquisition can equally easily be a help or a great hindrance to successful integration. The major specific functional areas of contact have been discussed before, with dos and don'ts regarding establishing good working relationships. This chapter deals more generally with the staff/line relationships in a large corporation, and especially how to manage them with the newly acquired company.

Corporate headquarters needs staff expertise in order to provide for top management an independent and objective evaluation of group and division functional effectiveness. This applies to all functions: marketing, engineering, manufacturing, finance, and personnel.

This does not mean attempting to track and direct the day-to-day activities in the divisions. This is beyond the capability of any headquarters staff operation, notwithstanding various grandiose attempts from time to time to do just that with a large central staff. It does mean evaluation of the professionalism with which the division's functional activities are conducted.

In evaluating marketing work, for example, it is rating the effectiveness of the field sales effort: advertising and sales promotion work; field sales training programs; sales meetings for distributors and representatives; the degree of control that marketing/sales has over customer service; and its interfaces with application engineering and new product design.

In addition the central headquarters marketing staff has overall corporate responsibilities. It should be looking for new product or market areas in which it might be fruitful for the corporation to become involved. It should be influential in recommending the use of certain representatives and distributors in the field rather than others, both because of possible tie-ins with other divisions, and to try to ensure that the divisions utilize the best available representatives and distributors in their field. The headquarters marketing people should also take a leading role in suggesting acquisitions and evaluating interesting candidates.

The same kind of considerations apply to the headquarters people in manufacturing, finance, business planning, and personnel. They should provide leadership for high standards of functional performance throughout the corporation, advice and counsel to their functional counterparts in the divisions, and monitor and evaluate functional performance for top management.

Of all the functions, it is in engineering that it is most difficult to maintain any kind of meaningful central evaluation of divisional activities. This, of course, is because the degree of specialization required to be a top-notch engineer in one product line is great, and it takes a long time to achieve. It is impossible, therefore, for the headquarters engineering personnel to possess such expertise in all the range of product activities in which the corporation is engaged. However, the central engineering staff can regularly review the technology areas in which the corporation currently has competence and be on the lookout for new technology areas that might become important in the future.

It is the monitor and evaluate aspects of a central headquarters staff that offers the potential for considerable trouble between staff and line, and especially with a newly acquired company where people have not previously had to contend with staff looking over their shoulder.

Besides the knowledgeability of the staff people, the two critical determinants of whether the headquarters staff will be effective or not are its size, and the beliefs of the chief executive of the corporation concerning the staff role.

On size, Parkinson's Law works with a vengeance. Beyond a certain critical mass, a large corporation's headquarters staff tends to grow irrespective of the amount of useful work to be done. The staff make work for each other, of course, but worse, they make unnecessary work for the line people. Since there are so many of them it is not just the important things that receive staff attention. Eventually, no line matter is sufficiently insignificant to avoid receiving "help" from headquarters staff.

The role and attitude of the staff in all-important, and it will be directly determined by that of the chief executive. If the staff is expected to be helpful to the line operations and to avoid indulging in destructive criticism; and if tactful instruction of division people is paramount, rather than rushing back to headquarters with a list of division faults and failings, then the corporation as a whole will benefit mightily from staff/line interfacing. If, on the other hand, there exists an adversary relationship between headquarters staff and the line divisions, the corporation will lose immeasurably. Immeasurably because the waste of human resources thus created does not lend itself to profit and loss quantification. Those experiencing this kind of situation, however, will be well aware of the wreckage strewn about the corporation because of staff/line conflict.

Before considering the problems of a new acquisition thrust into contact with a corporate headquarters staff, let's look at what has happened with a maxi and a mini headquarters staff, and how they interface with line operations.

One of the largest headquarters staff operations of modern times in manufacturing industry has undoubtedly been ITT's. When Harold Geneen became president in 1959, he found a far-flung multi-national corporation, whose many subsidiary companies, most of them outside the United States, operated virtually independently. Geneen intended to integrate this kaleidoscope of companies and nationalities into a corporation that would be close-knit, centrally directed, and effective worldwide.

There was a small New York headquarters staff in existence at the time, but it was somnolent. Geneen proceeded with immense vigor to change both the size and sleep habits of the staff. He dismissed 20 of 25 vice presidents and then increased the New York staff personnel by ten times within 18 months. The added staff were functional people: financial, marketing, engineering, employee relations, organization, and planning personnel.

The program given Geneen, when the board brought him in, was to establish four area managements: North America, South America,

Europe, and Asia. The area managements would be responsible for all the ITT subsidiaries in their geographical area.

Well, of course, each of these area managements wanted its own staff, so the New York world headquarters staff growth was repeated at the four area headquarters. When I joined ITT in 1961 in Brussels, headquarters of the European area, the staff consisted of some 50 people. By mid-1964, when I returned to the States, the Brussels staff had grown to 300. In 1970, ITT European area headquarters peaked at some 700 people, occupying and overflowing a high-rise building that had been built solely for the staff.

After 1970, both world headquarters and the area staffs were reduced, but this was due to the onset of hard times, not to top management recognition of what monsters the staffs had become. Left alone, that is, if the boom 1960s had continued, there is little doubt that ITT's five headquarters staffs (the world and the four areas) would have continued to proliferate.

After the initial rush of functional people into the new staffs, there occurred a second wave of product managers, and their numbers became legion. Geneen decided that in addition to functional expertise at world headquarters he needed worldwide product line managers. Their job would be to "integrate" the relevant product activities in the subsidiaries all over the world, in order to obtain a rationalization of these product efforts, to avoid overlap and duplication of product programs. Basically a good idea, but the implementation!

To begin, Geneen hired a telecommunications expert at world headquarters to be worldwide product manager for telecommunications products, ITT's strongest business. As this hardworking and knowledgeable man began to gather the threads of ITT's telecommunications activities, the area managements saw the light. Each of the four areas hired their own product manager for telecommunications products. Geneen's initial one had become five, and four of the five weren't really interested in worldwide integration of telecommunications product activities, only in "what does my area get out of this," and protection of existing activities, whatever their value.

Seeing he had been quickly outgunned, the world headquarters product manager, no slouch at playing the staff game, then brought in telecommunications product sub-managers: one for switching systems, one for transmission systems, one for private telephone exchanges, one for military communications systems, one for large proposals, one special projects—you name it. The area managements could barely keep the pace, but they managed it. The mirror image of world headquarters product manager expansion appeared in all four area headquarters. Within two or three years there were some 50 telecommunications product line managers flailing around at the world and area headquarters and creating considerable havoc in the operating divisions. In addition, there now appeared assistants and assistants-to, technical experts, marketing experts, all to aid and advise the corps of telecommunications product line managers in their various and sundry tasks.

Besides telecommunications, ITT was engaged in quite a variety of other fields: consumer products, electronic components, automated post offices, commercial refrigeration equipment, and, later, hotels, insurance companies, food, and publishing. All of these activities, of course, "needed" their own set of product line managers at world headquarters and at the area headquarters, so they increased and multiplied to a mind-boggling extent throughout the 1960s.

The sheer mass of headquarters staff personnel created a very real problem for the operating divisions. Anyone who didn't directly experience the paralyzing degree of interference by ITT staff in normal divisional activities would have difficulty believing it. The parade of headquarters staff visitors to a division was unending: functional "experts," in manufacturing, marketing, engineering, personnel, finance. Product line managers of all sizes and shapes. They wanted first, education. "What kind of business are you in?" "Who are the competitors?" "What sales volume did you do last year?" Very few had taken the trouble to read your division's latest business plan, which spelled out in vast detail all those things. No, they wanted the general manager's time, or that of his chief lieutenants, for hours on end.

After education, the staff people got to the nub of what they wanted, namely, "What are your problems?" The general manager would outline his trouble areas, of which there are always some lulus, and then hopefully wait for a suggestion or two from the visiting expert. Alas, very few were offered. The headquarters man had what he needed. He returned to world or area headquarters and wrote a long report on the problems he had "discovered" at the division, invariably concluding that "wow, have they got a lot of trouble out there," and recommending that only massive intervention by staff could perhaps save the division from total disaster.

The line/staff relations in ITT degenerated rapidly because of the sheer number of staff looking for things to do, the deliberately vague division of responsibility and authority between staff and line people, and, most importantly, the role of staff as seen by Harold Geneen.

The president of ITT seemed consciously to foster an adversary relationship between the giant staffs and the operating divisions. He didn't say it just that way, but what he did say to his headquarters executives and in the large monthly operating committee meetings each month made the result inevitable.

Geneen wanted to avoid "surprises," meaning adverse financial results. He characterized it at one meeting thus: "I don't want some division general manager to get into his own private Viet Nam, and then one morning walk in and drop his resignation on my desk, leaving us to pick up the pieces." How were such surprises to be avoided? Since headquarters believed that division general managers couldn't be trusted to disclose real trouble, actual or brewing, the staff was to ferret out the problems.

With this charge, that is, find problems, the staff found a lot of them. Geneen's worries about surprises were translated roughly as: "The divisions are peopled almost entirely by nitwits, who at best are simply incompetent, but more likely are actively trying to sabotage their own operations. Their purpose is to embarrass us at headquarters, so we'd better get the rascals before they get us."

Sound nightmarish? It was, at least all through the 1960s and early 1970s. During any visit to New York headquarters, either world or North American, the comments of staff people, including top executives, seemed to indicate that the "enemy" most feared was ITT's own line division people, not competition, market conditions, or changing technologies.

Did this adversary relationship, the huge staff, the "uncovering" of problems the division managments were "trying to conceal," really prevent surprises for Harold Geneen? No. Even a cursory look at some of the really whopping disasters that have befallen ITT shows the ineffectiveness of that frantic and at bottom destructive approach. An extreme example, true, but extreme examples can be instructive.

At the other end of the scale, a mini–headquarters staff example, is General Instrument. Chairman and President Frank Hickey, a line operating man himself, has never been tempted by the elephantine headquarters staff syndrome.

A few days after joining General Instrument as a group vice president in 1970, I was taken to lunch by Hickey. He had given me a pile of memos and business plans to read, and over lunch asked if I had read a memo to him by the recently hired headquarters staff expert on industrial engineering. The memo proposed that GI hire 24 industrial engineers at New York headquarters, whose assignment would be to visit the operating divisions and show them where cost reductions could be obtained by better industrial engineering. The program would cost $800,000 per year but would result in cost reductions of many millions of dollars annually.

With a serious mien, Hickey asked "Can you resist a money making machine like that?" "Yes I can," I responded, "if we can find 24 good industrial engineers, they should be located permanently at the divisions, not just make visits from headquarters." Hickey laughed. "That's exactly the way I feel."

The General Instrument HQ staff was and is minuscule, but almost all of them are excellent in their field of expertise. Those who turned out not to be didn't last very long. Since the headquarters staff was kept small, they necessarily had to involve themselves in only the most important situations. This is a key advantage to a corporation of having a small headquarters staff. You can be more confident that the highest-priority issues and problems are the ones being worked on. There is not the make-work, find or invent problems, artificial crisis atmosphere that was encouraged at ITT.

The General Instrument staff was expected to pitch in and help with problem divisions, and there was remarkably little of the kind of continual harassment and backbiting of division people that seems endemic with a large headquarters staff. This was due primarily to Hickey's constructive attitude towards staff/line relationships, and secondly to the maturity and expertise of the GI headquarters staff people, who didn't need to attack division people in order to prove themselves useful to headquarters.

From the foregoing it should be clear how an acquired company should be treated by the staff people from the parent corporation. A helpful "let's pool our expertise together" approach, a "let's solve problems together" attitude, and a "maybe your experience will be useful to other divisions" mild flattery will do a great deal toward getting the relationships off to a good start.

Keeping them that way requires a resolutely fair-minded attitude on the staff people's part. Weaknesses are not to be ignored or papered over, of course. Scared cows will have to be kicked, or at least challenged. Some unpleasant truths will have to be pointed out to division people. But the golden rule here is: be frank and open with the division people, and then avoid gossiping when back at headquarters. Tell other headquarters people of division problems you know about only on a "need to know" basis, and never give headquarters a different version of the situation from the one that you reviewed with the division people while there.

How to begin with the new acquisition? Slowly. Don't allow a "march through" of all the elements of the headquarters staff, even though they will want to look at the new situation as soon as possible. Give the new entity breathing time between the waves of headquarters functional staff people who will have to appear. Financial and marketing/sales people from headquarters have the most urgent need to know, as explained in earlier chapters, so should have priority. They can then be followed shortly by business planning and personnel people. Then, in due course, and with no tremendous urgency, the headquarters experts in electronic data processing, manufacturing, engineering, can begin to put in an appearance and establish relationships. After that, the planning and implementing of any needed or desired changes in the division's existing operating procedures can proceed step by step as described in earlier chapters.

13

ADVICE FOR ACQUIRED PERSONNEL

AFTER A SUCCESSFUL ENTREPRENEUR sells his company to a large, multi-division corporation, what does he do? There are four basic paths he can follow.

First, take his millions and walk away, putting his energy and talents to work in other fields. This first route is taken by many former owners, despite real heartfelt pangs at leaving their "baby," because they prize their independence so highly. They can't see making the effort to adjust to having a boss. Further, a boss who has a staff of people who also will be looking over their shoulder, getting involved in the business, critiquing. So they march out with banners flying, proud of what they have accomplished, and hoping that the acquiring corporation will keep its new entity's good reputation intact.

Second, there are the entrepreneurs who want to have their cake (the price received for their company) and eat it too (continue to operate on their own as if nothing has changed). These former owners are of course going to be disillusioned. They then wax bitter when, as is inevitable, the corporate way of doing things impinges on their past prerogatives and freedom of action.

It has to be a mystery of our age why many entrepreneurs who sell their companies apparently really expect to be left alone afterward by the acquiring corporation. A really surprising exercise in self-delusion, since it is done by adult people who have proven themselves to be smart, tough, and realistic in building their companies. It is another mystery, and not edifying, why buying corporations frequently do assure the potential acquisition that it will indeed be left alone after coming into the fold. A grotesque sort of a mating dance then takes place between acquirer and acquiree, with many mutual endearments exchanged with fervor, but the morning after the consummation of the marriage all "no interference" talk disappears. The acquirer knows it will happen, the acquiree certainly should know, yet sometimes both pretend that nothing will change.

The third group consists of those who are so dedicated to their companies that they want to continue to run them after the acquisition, even recognizing that their life will be much different. If they want to continue heading their companies, why then do they sell? Usually to convert fixed assets into liquid ones, for the benefit of themselves and their families, and for estate reasons.

They are willing to accept, though reluctantly, the restraints associated with a large corporation: increased paperwork in every aspect of the business for reporting and explaining; formal business planning; headquarters staff wandering around kicking the tires; going hat-in-hand to headquarters to seek approval of capital expenditures and operating budgets.

Understandably, this group finds the going rough, and somewhere along the line, usually sooner than later, most of them throw in the towel. It can be the umpteenth time their day is wasted by someone new from headquarters staff wanting to learn about the business, asking simple-minded or presumptuous questions. It could be the new headquarters planning vice president asking whether the corporation should be in their line of business at all. It might follow an ego-damaging critique of the division's performance by the responsible group manager or the president. For many reasons, most of the "I want to stay with my company" entrepreneurs do step out within a year or two after the acquisition.

Those few who do manage to survive the culture shock of transition from independent company president to division manager in a large corporation are extremely valuable people. As you would expect, they are a superior breed of manager within the corporation. They know their business in a nuts-and-bolts way that very few corporate-trained managers can even remotely approach.

Of chief significance, they have headed their business for 15 or 20 years or more, whereas many corporate general managers might spend only 3 or 4 years as head of a division before being transferred up, sideways, or out. The entrepreneurs know every facet of their operation, from the shop floor through engineering, sales, finance, and personnel. They know and visit their chief customers. They personally conduct labor union contract negotiations. They have been in all the chairs, so have a superb, down-to-earth grasp of what goes on all through the company. Also, most successful entrepreneurs are superior people: usually personally charming, always highly intelligent and energetic. They are winners.

Therefore, the new parent corporation who can keep the selling entrepreneur in the fold does itself a great service. Handling the initial interfaces with the new entity in such a manner as to minimize the inevitable conflicts and frustrations is a good way to try.

The final class of entrepreneurs is those who don't want to leave but who don't want the continuing headaches of running the business on a day-to-day basis either. They would like an elder statesman role, a senior consultant situation, certainly for their acquired company now a division, and if possible for the parent corporation. A seat on the corporate board suits them just fine.

If such an arrangement can be made, with this approach the entrepreneur neatly finesses any future critiquing from headquarters staff. *He* will do the critiquing, from his board seat or senior consultant position. Since most entrepreneurs have very favorable opinions of their own abilities, they will not limit their activities in their new role to their former company. They will be happy to advise and counsel the corporation generally on whatever is of interest at the moment.

This kind of entrepreneur is a mixed blessing. On the plus side he can provide useful insights for the corporate top management, expecially if he is a broad-gauged individual who is knowledgeable beyond his former company's particular field. On the minus side, he can be a decided pain to the people now responsible for operating his former company. Relieved of responsibility for the new division's financial performance, he can let himself go in telling all and sundry what the new manager should be doing, and recounting again and again how he did it in the good old days.

The case histories of three entrepreneurs I have worked with will illustrate the general comments above. Bob Cannon, Ernie Freeman, and Carl Clare were alike in that they each built up a family-owned business to the point where it became the leader in its particular products, successfully growing while contending with competitors of all sizes. All three were absolutely top-class business executives, who could have gone to the top in almost any corporate environment. They also all eventually sold their companies to large multi-division corporations. And there the similarity ends. Let's look at what happened after their companies were acquired, to illustrate the basic routes an entrepreneur can take.

Bob Cannon was the president of Cannon Electric, Los Angeles, the premier producer of multi-contact connectors in both the United States and Europe. The company, founded by Bob's father, had grown greatly during the 17 years the younger Cannon managed it.

In the early 1960s Cannon's brother and two sisters, coowners of the business that Bob was managing, pressed for selling the company. One sister had just moved from Los Angeles to San Jose and urged sale, saying, "I'm supposed to be rich, but my husband and I can't even afford the down payment on the house we want to buy!"

After unanimous family agreement to sell Cannon to the most qualified high bidder was achieved, Bob looked around for a suitable purchaser. A big one was right at hand in Los Angeles, Litton. Litton, under Tex Thornton and Roy Ash, was flying high and making acquisitions right and left, and it wooed Cannon assiduously. So why didn't Litton succeed in buying Cannon? "Aw, I really didn't want to sell to Litton," Bob Cannon said. "I see those guys all the time!"

Enter International Telephone and Telegraph, also making numerous acquisitions. With corporate headquarters 3000 miles away in New York, ITT looked better to Cannon than Litton next door. The sale was completed in 1963 for 32 million dollars, one-fourth each to Bob Cannon and his brother and two sisters. It can be safely presumed that a San Jose home down payment was no longer a problem.

What were Bob Cannon's plans? He told me he had made up his mind to step out following completion of the acquisition. "Hell," Bob said, "I could get along with anybody, even Geneen, but why should I try? I've taken this company through 17 years of up-and-down struggle. It is now the largest supplier anywhere of multi-contact connectors—the premier name in the industry. But I can't see myself putting up with ITT's brand of corporate Mickey Mouse. I've got a lot of other projects I'm interested in spending my time on, so I'm leaving."

When I arrived in Los Angeles for Brussels as the new head of the now ITT Cannon Electric, Bob Cannon, a perfect gentleman, smoothed the way by indicating to the Cannon peopel his complete approval of the new relationship. He told me, "I'll be glad to consult with you any time you ask, but I won't be calling you. Good luck, and keep the Cannon halo shining." Then he turned over his office to me and left.

Afterward, always at my request, he did enter the plant several times to discuss the business. But there was none of the second-guessing, criticizing from the sidelines, undercutting the new bosses, that all too often a selling entrepreneur indulges in after he has stepped out.

Bob Cannon's way of leaving the Cannon Electric that he had built up so beautifully over so many hard-fought years was a class act. It is a model for selling entrepreneurs who, for whatever reason, don't want to continue operating their businesses in the large corporate environment.

For a perfect example of the entrepreneur who wants to continue heading the business after acquisition, consider Ernie Freeman of Chicago Miniature Lamp. CML had been founded by Freeman's father-in-law, who prevailed upon Ernie to take over the business just after World War II. Ernie had then found and carefully developed a special niche for his Chicago Miniature Lamp Company in very small incandescent lamps. In this narrow product segment he ran rings around the giants—General Electric, Westinghouse, Sylvania—and had become the largest supplier of such lamps in the United States when he sold the company to General Instrument in 1969.

At the time Freeman was still operating his company with the same intensity as when he started some 25 years earlier, and he had no intention of turning the helm over to anyone else. CML was an excellent example of a small company whose head man knew his business backward and forward; kept his own counsel; made his calculations on the backs of old envelopes; operated strictly on a cash basis; squeezed every possible dime out of expenses; and generally had an operation stretched to an alarming degree of tightness.

Since he wanted to continue operating the business, why did Freeman sell? "We had reached the point," he told me, "where large capital expenditures needed to be made for new, faster equipment. I was unwilling to borrow to do it. We had never been in debt to anyone, and I wasn't going to start now. Also, I was 60 and had to start thinking about estate tax problems if I died with so much of the family's assets tied up in the business."

So Chicago Miniature Lamp, with its entrepreneur still heading the business, entered the General Instrument family of divisions. Faced with the full panoply of large corporation requirements of their subsidiaries, Ernie was astonished, even though he thought he was prepared for it. The reality was worse and more complicated than perusal of the *Harvard Business Review*, which Ernie had read for years, would lead one to expect.

"The worst part," he said, "is the time, the hours, the days required to produce things that help our business not at all but are wanted by headquarters. I'm glad to discuss, or write about, anything that Monte Shapiro (then chairman) or Frank Hickey (then president) requests. In fact I welcome their interest in our little operation. But it's all those other guys in the picture that are hard to take: a financial analyst wanting me to explain to him our manufacturing variances last month; a legal guy inquiring whether we've broken any laws lately; seemingly never ending questions about our capital expenditure requests. For example, about our needed new faster carousels for making lamps. Our old equipment is now hopelessly outdated. We're holding it together with rubber bands and chewing gum. So a guy in the controller's office at headquarters wants to know why we don't increase capacity by just running more shifts, instead of buying more machinery. It isn't that the questions are dumb—they're not. It's that they take up so much time that we used to spend entirely on making and selling lamps."

Despite the irritations and frustrations, Ernie persisted, and persisted, as operating head of Chicago Miniature Lamp. Why? One important reason was that General Instrument kept Monte Shapiro's promise to Freeman that the corporation would spend the capital money necessary to modernize and reequip CML's plant. In return, Ernie felt that he could and should deliver good earnings and cash to the corporation, and he did so, year after year.

Also, remarkably quickly, he mastered the new environment and successfully played the game by General Instrument rules. His financial reports were always complete and made on time; his manager's letters were models, written with clarity, sense of humor, and occasional pithy earthiness when he became too irritated by what he saw as faults and failings of the corporate headquarters people. At review and planning meetings with headquarters brass, Freeman invariably carried the day with irresistible panache, based solidly on superior knowledge of his customers, competitors, and internal operations, and all presented with lively good humor, as well as patient consideration of differing or naive viewpoints.

Freeman ranks high in the personal pantheon of business heroes I've worked with, and he never did quit leadership of his company Ernie died with his boots on, and his untimely departure was regretted by all.

The third entrepreneur to illustrate the career paths available after acquisition is Carl Clare, founder of the C. P. Clare Company. C. P. Clare is the world's largest producer, after Western Electric, of sophisticated sealed reed relays, used for telecommunications, process control, and computer peripheral equipment.

Carl founded the company in 1937 and built it up with remarkable vision of future relay requirements, superlative engineering, and quality manufacturing. Unfortunately from Clare's standpoint, he had from the beginning a majority partner, the American Totalisator Company, brought in to supply capital when Carl started his company.

Unfortunately, because the American Totalisator owner sold it, along with its majority ownership of the Clare Company, when Carl Clare himself was not really in favor of being acquired by anyone. "The greatest mistake of my life," he told me, "was not to buy American Totalisator myself. It was offered to me at a price I could have raised, borrowing against my company and my personal assets. But I didn't want to be that much is debt, and my equally conservative banker advised against it. I've regretted not doing it ever since."

General Instrument acquired American Totalisator and C. P. Clare in 1969. At that time, Carl Clare, already over 65, though holding the titles of chairman and president, had stopped managing the day-to-day operations of his company. In the relay industry he had evolved into a well-earned elder statesman, admired and respected by customers and competitors alike.

C. P. Clare was important enough in the General Instrument portfolio at the time, and Carl Clare's reputation was such, that he was elected to a seat on the corporate board. The Clare division's day-to-day management was in the hands of an intelligent and charming man, but one totally unprepared to accept operating and reporting in the mode required by General Instrument. Thus, with Carl Clare, the possessor of a normal successful entrepreneur's large ego, on GI's board, while his namesake company, now a division, had a general manager unsuited for the more onerous and rigorous management style demanded by the parent corporation, the stage was set for conflict.

The internal warfare that evolved took a two-level form. At the board and top executive level, Clare rejected any question about, or criticism of, the Clare division's performance, which in fact was sliding downhill. He counterattacked vigorously, pointing to other underachieving divisions as much more in need of headquarters attention, and maintaining that all would be well at the Clare division if only it was left alone.

At the Clare division operations, the most destructive kind of local management resistance to the new corporate parent took place. General Instrument was openly described to lower-level employees as untrustworthy, somehow intent on destroying the C. P. Clare company reputation, stealing the Clare profit-sharing funds, and generally causing havoc out of sheer meanness of spirit. Policies and procedures arriving from GI headquarters were uniformly greeted as unnecessary wastes of time and tossed to subordinates with not even a halfhearted attempt to explain or support. The manager's letters and business plans required by the corporation were given cursory treatment and turned out to be just window dressing.

In fairness, it is also true that some of Clare's most fondly cherished sacred cows were kicked around more roughly than a wise acquirer should permit. This ranged from a too vigorous prosecutorial approach by Chairman Monte Shapiro, intended to bring Clare quickly up to snuff, down to counterproductive harassment by various headquarters people who ignored the good acquirer guidelines described in this book.

As the General Instrument vice president put in charge of Clare and two other divisions in 1971, I arrived at the Chicago headquarters and conferred with Carl Clare in the palatial office he still maintained there, just down the hall from the division manager's office. Carl was blunt in his appraisal of the parent corporation. The essence of his comments was: "We don't trust General Instrument. The tract record is bad. Nobody likes the corporation. The poor reputation of other divisions is hurting Clare." He saw little hope for the future unless General Instrument top brass acknowledged their errors and got into step with the Clare division.

What really was the Clare situation? An ongoing business that was number one in its field of sealed relays, as Cannon was in connectors. A company built up by an exceptionally able entrepreneur over many years. But a company that had become complacent, self-satisfied, even arrogant. And it was slipping. The founder couldn't see this, especially since he no longer managed the business, but it was clear enough to customers, competitors, and many competent Clare people.

Painful changes had to be made, and they were, but the story has a happy ending for this entrepreneur. Once he became convinced that there were very real Clare division problems that should be addressed, Carl withdrew from active opposition and let the new management do its work unhindered.

Then, when Frank Hickey became president of General Instrument, Carl Clare came into a new golden age at 75. Frank appreciated Carl's technical expertise and wide-ranging business interests and began utilizing him not only on the board, but also to provide advice and counsel to other GI operations from time to time. Thus, from a very rocky beginning, Clare was now accepted by General Instrument's top man as an elder statesman with a lot to contribute to the corporation. No one today is more enthusiastic about General Instrument than Carl P. Clare.

Thus three case histories of acquired entrepreneurs. The common denominator is that their business lives changed drastically following sale of their companies to larger corporations. This will happen to any acquisition's people. There is now a much larger group of participants in the game, new ground rules to be learned, a different environment. Will the changed ambience be one of cooperative or adversary relationships?

Much of the foregoing presentation of the proper handling of integrating acquisitions successfully into a larger corporation has focused on the faults and failings of the acquirer. A rough rule of thumb is that 75 percent of the problems after acquisition are caused by the acquirer. But what about the other 25 percent?

The single most glaring and trouble-causing fault in an acquired company almost always stems directly from its top managers. This is the deliberate creation of an "us vs. them" atmosphere toward the new parent. Everything that comes from the parent is resisted, criticized, ridiculed. Installing any of the necessary new systems and procedures is objected to, delayed, even sabotaged. Policy statements from the corporate HQ are misinterpreted, mangled out of recognition, before being passed on to subordinates.

Other operations of the corporation are compared to those of the new acquisition and invariably found wanting. Problems in sister divisions, or at corporate HQ, are greeted with ill-concealed glee, rather than sympathetic understanding.

The standard answer to any question from HQ people is, "Look, you don't know our business. We do. Just leave us alone and let us do things our way." Or, "Why are you talking to us? We happen to know that x division is in serious trouble. Go 'help' them." Or, "You know, our people don't trust Omega Corporation." All things that, of course, do not create a warm glow in the HQ people, who have jobs to do that *require* their active interfacing with the new entity. The result: acrimony, mutual recriminations, a waste of everyone's time and energy.

Sometimes the latent antagonism is made starkly clear at the beginning. At the time of Cannon's acquisition by ITT, Bob Cannon recommended that his engineering vice president be made the new president when Bob left. Geneen agreed. Then the president designate, a man of vast self-confidence, wrote a letter to ITT's president. This remarkable document informed Geneen that ITT knew nothing of the connector business, whereas the writer knew everything. Further, that he was not impressed with what he had seen of ITT, and, in fact, did not trust the new parent corporation. Accordingly, the letter continued, he must now have a written guarantee from Geneen himself that he would have a completely free hand to operate Cannon as he saw fit, and not be interfered with in any way by HQ. The letter closed with a demand for a five-year written contract for himself, at a salary far above what he was then earning.

Geneen's reaction? Predictable, decisive, but verbally rather mild. He simply said, "That man may be the world's greatest in the connector industry, but I can't accept a letter like this." So the heir was out even before starting in on his inheritance.

More often the antagonism is less blatant, better concealed from HQ people. It is expressed in local meetings within the acquired entity, over business lunches, at social gatherings. What is the reasoning of those executives in an acquired company who deliberately place themselves in an adversary position vis-à-vis the new parent?

On the surface it appears that they somehow expect to bolster their position by appealing to narrow local interests, believing that their stature will be enhanced locally by representing themselves as defenders of the local people, battling desperately against the forces of evil represented by the HQ people of the parent corporation. But whatever their reasons, they invariably end by being crushed. Since their only source of support is local, they inevitably lose out sooner or later to the bombardment thrown their way by outraged HQ people. The downfall is hastened, of course, should P & L performance slip.

The pettiness and, yes, vindictiveness of some "adversary" executives in acquired companies is truly surprising. Examples: a letter to customers stating that actions being taken, raising prices, say, or eliminating a product line, have been "ordered by our new parent corporation"; or statements to customers, or to a plant union, that "we can no longer guarantee performance according to contract, since we have been acquired by Omega Corporation"; statements to employees that their jobs are threatened because of the acquisition, or that benefit plans will be reduced; even malicious gossip regarding the honesty and morals of the acquiring company's chief officers.

This is an unpleasant aspect of acquisitions, and it must be dealt with forcefully by the acquirer, that is, by removing the offenders wherever they are found. No matter how capable an executive the "adversary"man is, he must be eliminated from the organization. His brand of poison is more harmful to the overall health of the company than any benefits he might produce through individual brilliance.

For the great majority of the acquired company's employees, the acquisition can represent opportunity, so they should keep an open mind toward the new parent. If the company you work for is one built up and still run by an entrepreneur, and one day you learn it has been sold to a large corporation, consider these aspects.

The owner did not sell without a reason. Perhaps age or health problems prevent him from carrying on the battle with the necessary vigor. Maybe he sees things ahead for the company, or its industry, that spell big trouble. Perhaps he wants to convert his fixed assets in the business to liquid assets for himself and his family. He may even have "retired in office" some time ago, and been just waiting for a chance to sell out at a good price.

In any event, you can be sure of one thing. He is considering his own best interests when he sells, not yours. Most successful entrepreneurs are takers, not givers. You can respect his accomplishments. You can admire the way he handles people and business problems. You can think he's a great guy. Just don't make the mistake of sentimentalizing the sale of the company as another little guy "losing out" to a large corporation. That leads to automatically casting the new corporate parent as the bad guy, and to viewing with suspicion the HQ people you will meet and have to work with.

It's very easy to slip into an "us vs. them" attitude, following acquisition. Rumors will abound, most of them unfavorable to the new parent, some entirely outrageous. Yet asking a few questions at the acquired division is sufficient to reveal that the people making these statements know next to nothing about the new parent corporation. So where does this attitude originate? It is sad, but true, that most of it comes from the key executives left behind by the former owner's departure, who somehow hope to preserve independence and believe that fostering an "it's us against them" atmosphere will be useful.

It doesn't work, of course. No corporation is going to spend multi-millions of dollars to acquire a company, and then walk away and leave it alone, whatever the objections from the acquired company's people to HQ involvement. It doesn't work, but the deliberate creation of "us vs. them" does an immense amount of harm.

Don't participate in it. It is ultimately harmful to your best interests and is, at bottom, cowardly. It is a hit-and-run attempt to sabotage people you don't even know, before you can judge them on their merits.

Rather, realize that the acquisition broadens your horizons. There are a lot more jobs in a large corporation, interesting jobs, and managerial positions. Keep in mind too that the search for talent in a large corporation is intense. Good people are needed. They want you!

All through the corporation people are always changing: because of retirements, deaths, health problems, and yes, dismissals. Reorganizations take place, creating opportunities. There will be in-house training programs, opportunities to broaden your experience through transfers, perhaps an international assignment.

You will have plenty of opportunities to shine in the new environment, to show promise, to produce good results, and if you do, you will progress. Don't worry about your light being hidden under the bushel of an acquired company. It will be noticed. Of course, the competition is tougher than in the small company, if only because there is more of it. But there are also many more opportunities for advancement.

Therefore, from the beginning avoid the "us vs. them" attitude. This doesn't mean fawning over the corporate people you meet. Far from it; just be yourself.

The corporate HQ people may seem to you to be forever saying, "We at Omega Corporation do it this way." If so, notice how often you and your divisional colleagues seem to be saying "Well, at Alpha Company we do it that way."

Should you disagree with corporate people when you think they're off base? Definitely. Don't hesitate to make your points with anyone when a serious business situation is being discussed. The better people from HQ will respect you for it. The "bad" HQ staff type may hasten back and report that you are "uncooperative," but no life is without some risk. Bet with confidence on good HQ people, and keep on contributing to your division and the corporate welfare.

The opportunities you will have to speak directly to the top executives of the parent corporation will, no doubt, be few, but they are important. Be prepared! Know your points of discussion backward and forward, and speak with authority. If your local boss manages quietly, seldom raising his voice, and the new corporate bigwig turns out to be a screamer, don't panic. He may well turn out to be a good and fair man, despite the histrionics. If you're used to a loud boss, and the new Ms. Big from HQ is serious and quiet, don't underestimate her.

The golden rule is: be yourself, and concentrate on the job to be done. Deal with your new colleagues fairly and naturally, and the acquisition may well turn out to be your springboard to great business success.

INDEX

acquired entrepreneurs: alternatives, 148-50; value 150

acquisitions: effect on customers, 124-25, 128-29; integration problems of finance 5-6, 7-10, electronic data processing, 16, 18-19, marketing/sales 32-35, 37, 38-39, 41-42, manufacturing 50-55, public relations 118-19, 124, in business planning 109-12, international operations 61-69, personnel policies 21-22, with consultants 131-33; minimizing integration problems of finance 7-8, 9-10, electronic data processing 18-20, engineering 49, manufacturing 56-57, 59-60, marketing/sales 32-35, 36, 38-40, 43, public relations 119, 120-21, personnel policies 23-30, with consultants 133-37, in business planning 115-16, use of staff 146-47; synergism aspects of 74-76, 78-86

advertising, 43, 121-23

aircraft instruments, 102-03

Air France, 99

Allied Corp., 74-76, 94

American Bosch, 128-29

American Totalisator, 127-28, 154

area management, 69-71, 143-44

Ash, Roy, 151

auditors: internal, 6; external 137-38, 139

automatic wagering equipment, 78

Bank of America, 27-30, 100

Belgium, 65, 77

Bell & Gossett, 126-27

Bell Telephone Mfg. (BTM), 100

Bendix, 74-76, 93-94

Boeing, 38, 122

Booz, Allen, Hamilton, 93, 130

Boston Consulting Group, 111, 130, 135-36

Brussels, 143

Burroughs, 19, 101

business planning: acquirer's mistakes, 54, 112-14, 115; development of, General Electric 106-08, General Instrument 108-09, ITT 108; difficulty of, 105-06; integrating the acquisition, 109-12; importance of, 105, 115; minimizing the acquisition's problems, 116; strategic, 111, 134-36

cable television 43,74, 78

calculators, 77

Cannon Electric, 22, 126-27, 151-52

Cannon, Robert, 150-52, 157

Charles Schwab, 30

Chicago, 155
Chicago Miniature Lamp, 28, 128, 152-53
Clare, Carl P., 150, 154-56
C. P. Clare Co., 27-28, 38, 59, 87, 127-28, 138, 154-56
Clare International, 77-78
Common Market, 66
computers, 12-20, 49, 99-101
Conoco, 94, 125
consultants: acquisition's problems with, 131-33; executive search, 136-37; minimizing acquisition problems, 133-37, strategic business planning 135-36; use of, 48, 130-131, 133-36
Control Data, 101
Cordiner, Ralph, 100, 106-107
corporate entrepreneurs: line initiatives, 97-102; problems for acquisitions, 95-98; staff initiatives, 88-92; top executive ventures, 90-95
corporate staff: at General Instrument, 145-46, at ITT, 144-45; minimizing acquisition's problems, 146-47; size, 142-44; use of, 140-147

Datapoint, 77
Deloitte, Haskins, and Sells, 139
Delorain, Maurice, 100
distributors, 32, 34-35, 37, 38-39, 41-42, 71
duPont, 94, 125

electronic data processing: financial use, 13; integration problems of, 15-16, 18-19; management understanding of, 16-17; manufacturing use, 13; minimizing integration difficulties, 18-20; myths of control, 12-13; organization of, 13-14, 17-18, 19-20
engineering: competence in, 44-45; evaluation of, 44, 46-48, 50; importance of, 45, 48-49; minimizing integration difficulties, 49; mistakes of, 45-46
European Economic Community, 66
executive perquisites, 27-30
Exxon, 92-93, 125

finance: integration problems, 5-6, 7-10; international operations difficulties 63-66; minimizing the acquisition's problems, 7, 9-11
Freeman, Ernest, 150, 152-54

Geneen, Harold, 22, 47, 67, 70, 99-100, 108, 114, 126-27, 142-45, 157
General Controls, 37, 126
General Electric: 46, 48-49, 92, 102, 123; aircraft instruments, 102-03; computers, 48-49, 100-01; instrument transformers, 45, 86; lightning arresters, 45; management school, 48; power transformers, 46; switchgear, 86; watt-hour meters, 102-03
General Instrument: 14-15, 27, 59, 74, 80, 108-09, 127-28, 145-47; cable television, 43; calculators, 76-77; keyboards, 76; light emitting diodes, 101-02; microelectronics, 76, 77-78; relays, 38-39

Harvard Business Review, 153
Harvard Business School, 132
Hennessy, Edward, 76

Hewlett-Packard, 102
Hickey, Frank, 43, 77, 80, 108, 128,
    145-46, 153, 156
Hilton Hotels, 36
Honeywell, 16, 19, 37, 94, 101

instrument transformers, 45
Intel, 94
internal selling, 75, 78-79, 83-87
International Business Machines
    (IBM), 16, 19, 101
international operations: basic prob-
    lems of, 61-73; distributors, 71;
    finance, 64-65; language, 62-63;
    local management, 72; nation-
    alism, 63, 66, 73; ombudsman,
    72; personnel policies, 67-69;
    sales, 66-67; scope of, 61
International Telephone and Tele-
    graph (ITT), 22, 41, 47, 67-68,
    70, 109, 126-27, 142-45, 151, 157

Jerrold, 74, 127-28
Jet Engines, 74

keyboards, 76-77, 78

lawyers, 137-38
light emitting diodes (LEDS), 101-02
Le Matériel Téléphonique (LMT), 99
lightning arresters, 46
Litton Industries, 151
Lockheed, 122
Los Angeles, 151

Magnavox, 94
management: area vs. product line,
    69-71, 143; matrix 70, 81
Machines Bull, 101
manufacturing: acquisition effect on,
    51-55; capital expenditures of,

58-60; complexity of 50, 57-58;
    minimizing integration difficul-
    ties of 56-57, 59-60; in business
    planning, 54-57; multi-division
    factories, 80-81
marketing: evaluation of, 38-41; im-
    portance of, 31; integration dif-
    ficulties of, 32-35, 37, 38-39,
    41-42; internal selling, 83-87;
    minimizing acquisition prob-
    lems, 32-35, 36, 38-40, 43;
    organization of, 33-34, 35-36, 81
Martin Marietta, 94
matrix management, 70, 81
McDonnell-Douglas, 122
Merrill, Lynch, Pierce, Fenner &
    Smith, 118
metal oxide silicon microchips, 76,
    77, 78, 114
Mexico, 56
microelectronics, 77, 78, 114
Mobil, 125
Monsanto, 101-02

National Semiconductor, 48
NCR, 77, 101
not invented here (NIH), 45, 48, 89,
    96
Noyce, Robert, 48

organization: area management,
    69-71, 142; in marketing/sales,
    33, 35-36, 80-81; in electronic
    data processing, 13-14, 17,
    19-20; matrix management, 70,
    81; product line management,
    69-71, 142-43

Parkinson's Law, 141
Peat, Marwick, Mitchell, 139

ABOUT THE AUTHOR

JAMES A. YUNKER is a consultant and retired business executive. For ten years, until 1981, he was a senior vice-president and group general manager of the General Instrument Corporation.

During his industrial career, Mr. Yunker was responsible for integrating and managing nine new or recent acquisitions, seven in the United States and two in Europe.

Mr. Yunker was a division and group general manager during seven years with ITT, including three years resident in Europe. Earlier, during thirteen years with General Electric, he held general management, engineering, manufacturing, and marketing positions. Mr. Yunker also served two years as chairman and president of Astrodata, Inc. He holds a BSEE degree from the University of Louisville, Kentucky.